SURVIVORS

SURVIVORS

True Stories
of
Children
in the
Holocaust

Allan Zullo and Mara Bovsun

SCHOLASTIC INC.

New York   Toronto   London   Auckland   Sydney
Mexico City   New Delhi   Hong Kong   Buenos Aires

To the Novodor family, especially Alice,
who will always remain a part of my soul
— A.Z.

To Michael, who taught me the importance
of remembering our history lessons
— M.B.

ISBN 0-439-66996-0

36 35 34 33 32 31 30 29 28 27 26   14 15 /0

Printed in the U.S.A.   40

First Scholastic printing, September 2004

www.allanzullo.com

Acknowledgments

We wish to extend our heartfelt gratitude to the survivors featured in this book for their willingness to relive, in interviews with us, the painful and emotional memories of their experiences as children so many years ago.

We also want to thank the following: Lore Baer, the Hidden Child Foundation, New York (**www.adl.org/hidden/start.asp**); the Museum of Jewish Heritage, New York (**www.mjhnyc.org**); Scott Miller, the United States Holocaust Memorial Museum, Washington, D.C. (**www.ushmm.org**); Debi Miles, the Center for Diversity Education, Asheville, North Carolina (**www.main.nc.us/diversity**); and Eva Floersheim, Lower Galilee, Israel, the Missing Identity Project (**www.jewishgen.org/missing-identity**).

Authors' Note

You are about to read eight incredible true stories of nine brave young survivors of the Holocaust. The names, dates, and places are real. Their stories are based exclusively on the personal, lengthy interviews we conducted with each of them. The accounts are written as factual and truthful versions of the survivors' recollections, although some of the dialogue has been re-created.

Much of what appears in the following pages is disturbing and horrifying. Although the stories are often difficult to read, we have not attempted to soften them, because that is how they really happened. It's hard to imagine that anyone, especially children, could bear so much suffering.

Yet this book is also a celebration of the human spirit — the will to overcome unspeakable horrors, the will to triumph over evil, the will to live. In fact, the people in these stories all shared a common trait — they believed in their hearts that they would live even when so many others around them were dying. Not only did these children survive, they also grew up, got married, and have enjoyed happy, fulfilling lives.

Their experiences reveal that even in the most horrible and hopeless situations imaginable, young people can rely on their courage, their faith, their smarts — and sometimes, sheer luck — to pull them through.

We hope that you find the stories in this book inspiring, and that they help you to understand how important it is to keep recalling the past . . . so no one ever forgets.

Allan Zullo and
Mara Bovsun

Contents

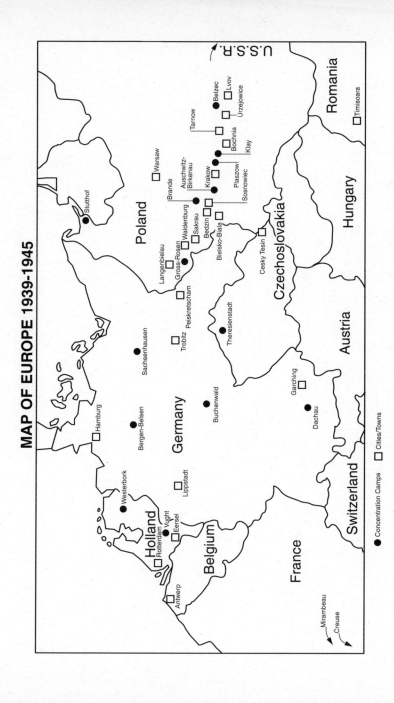

The Holocaust

Led by dictator Adolf Hitler, the Nazi Party in Germany in the 1930s and 1940s believed that certain people — particularly Jews, Gypsies, homosexuals, and the disabled — were inferior and didn't deserve to live.

The Nazis were anti-Semitic, which means they hated Jews. Although many Jews were doctors, lawyers, businesspeople, bankers, and teachers who contributed a great deal to German society, Hitler blamed them for Germany's economic problems. The truth was that Germany was going through a difficult time economically because it had been badly defeated in World War I, which had ended in 1918.

Hitler and his parliament passed laws that required Jews to give up their jobs, their homes, their businesses, and their rights. To enforce these laws, the police organization known as the Gestapo and an elite army corps known as the SS imprisoned, beat, and even murdered Jews — simply because they were Jewish. Non-Jews who opposed the Nazis' authority suffered similar treatment. Many Jews and political enemies of the Nazis were sent to brutally run prisons known as concentration camps.

Hitler was determined to protect at all costs "German blood and German honor" for the country's Aryans, the name given to white, non-Jewish Germans. He was also determined to invade and take control of *all* of Europe.

In March 1938, Germany conquered Austria and enacted harsh new laws stripping Austrian Jews of their rights. Then, in September 1939, German troops invaded Poland. This caused Great Britain and France, who were allies of Poland, to declare war on Germany, thus triggering the start of World War II. The following year, Nazi forces invaded and occupied the European nations of Denmark, Norway, Belgium, Holland, and Luxembourg. Then France fell, and Great Britain was battered by German air assaults. In December 1941, the United States entered the war and joined the Soviet Union (which included Russia), Great Britain, and the Free French (an organization fighting for the liberation of France) to form the Allied forces, which battled to stop the German war machine.

Also fighting the Nazis in German-occupied territory were secret groups of brave citizens known as the underground, the Resistance, or the Partisans. They used sabotage against the German army and helped Jews escape. In addition, courageous non-Jews (known typically in the Jewish community as Righteous Gentiles) risked their lives to save Jews from the Nazis.

As country after country fell under German occupation, Jews were singled out for mistreatment and lost their rights. They had to wear the six-pointed Star of David, a symbol of Judaism, on their sleeves, chests, or backs to distinguish them from non-Jews. They couldn't walk freely in the streets or do many of the things Europeans took for granted. Signs in theaters, cafés, restaurants, and other public places warned that Jews weren't allowed to enter.

During the war years, the Nazis created ghettos — small sealed areas inside cities where Jews were forced to live in unhealthy and crowded conditions. Every month, tens of thousands of Jews were deported to forced-labor camps, concentration camps, and death camps, where, unless they were useful to the Nazis, they were killed in gas chambers or murdered in some other way. It was all part of Hitler's "Final Solution" — the Nazi plan to eliminate all the Jews of Europe.

As the war came to an end in 1945, the Allies liberated the imprisoned Jews, although hundreds of thousands were barely alive because of Nazi cruelty. The world was shocked to discover that of the 9 million Jews who had lived in Europe before the war, 6 million had been murdered or had died from starvation or disease in Nazi camps. Another 4 million civilians, including 3 million Polish Catholics, died at the hands of the Nazis. Of the Jewish children who failed to escape Europe after 1939, more than a million and a half were murdered by the Nazis or were deported to camps, where they died of illness or hunger.

This horrific mass murder is called the Holocaust, a word derived from ancient Greek and meaning "sacrifice by fire."

Out of the ashes of the Holocaust emerged a new country — Israel — where in 1948 hundreds of thousands of Jews started a new life free from the tyranny of hate. Many other Holocaust survivors chose to remain in Europe, come to America, or settle in other continents, hoping to pick up the pieces of their shattered lives. They each had a story to tell, but over the decades the world still has heard too few of them. Now, with each passing year, the number of Holocaust survivors dwindles as they pass on from old age.

Their stories deserve to be told before it is too late.

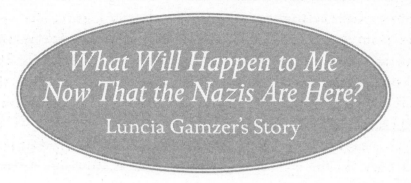

What Will Happen to Me Now That the Nazis Are Here?
Luncia Gamzer's Story

Luncia Gamzer jerked awake when the night erupted in angry shouts and screams of terror coming from the street below.

"*Tatu*, what's happening?" Luncia whimpered from her bedroom.

"Go back to bed," her father ordered from the living room, as he peeked out the window through the curtains. "You don't need to see this."

Luncia was too young to understand that the chaos outside on this frightening summer night in 1941 had been triggered by Germany's invasion and occupation of the Polish city of Lvov. Until a few days earlier, Luncia's hometown had been under the control of the Soviet Union. Now, at the urging of the Nazis, locals known as

Ukrainian nationalists were ransacking Jewish-owned stores and the homes of Jewish families in Lvov.

A mob was attacking an apartment building across the street from the one where eight-year-old Luncia lived with her parents, Isaac and Barbara. The intruders were smashing dishes and crystal and throwing furniture out the window.

Luncia covered her head with her pillow, hoping to drown out the cries of anguish and the shattering of glass that filled the night air. Unable to muffle the sounds of horror, she bolted out of bed and joined her parents in the living room. But when she looked in their eyes, she felt even more scared. They didn't say a word. The tension was too much.

"Are they going to come here, *Tatu*?" Luncia finally asked.

"No, I don't think so, kitten," Luncia's father said. Turning to his wife, Isaac whispered, "Let us pray they don't."

The next morning, Luncia and her mother ventured across the street to visit their neighbors. "Do you see what those nationalists did?" wailed Mrs. Silber, her left arm in a makeshift sling. "The Nazis put them up to this. They smashed our furniture and broke every dish. They even destroyed the sink. Look, they broke my arm. And for what? Our only crime is that we're Jewish!"

Luncia squeezed her mother's hand. "Mama, *we're* Jewish," she whispered. "Are they going to do that to us?"

When her mother didn't offer a reply, Luncia knew the

answer. She understood that the life she had been living would never be the same.

She wondered how much longer she'd be able to walk freely down the tree-lined streets to her favorite place — the family's candy and pastry shop. She loved sniffing the sweet aroma of sugar boiling in the kettle and seeing her father make chocolates and rum balls and colorful lollipops shaped like flowers. For his cute, pint-sized daughter only, Isaac would make a special treat — a heart-shaped candy with a delicate sugary flower inside. "A sweet for my sweetie," he'd say.

Luncia thought about the big ice cream machine in the store's window and how much she enjoyed seeing the colors swirl when its brightly painted wheel spun around. Now that the Nazis were in control, she wondered, would the colors still seem so cheerful? For that matter, would the ice cream even taste as good?

Luncia wondered, too, how much longer Uncle Hersh would be able to come into the shop and say, as he always did, "Luncia, you need more meat on your bones, so have some ice cream with me." She'd always jump onto his lap and share a large cup with him.

She thought about her parents' employees, grumpy Frank Ojak and his wife, Lusia, and how the cranky baker was always shooing Luncia out of the store every time she swiped a piece of chocolate. Would he and Lusia still be making those yummy pastries, including the best Napoleons in town?

Would the non-Jewish customers still flock to the store

as they had in the past? Luncia wondered if she would still see the ones who often told her how charming and pretty she was, especially Irene Szczygiel. "You are like a living doll," Irene would tell Luncia. "And not too much bigger than one, either."

What will happen to me, Luncia wondered, *now that the Nazis are here?*

◈   ◈   ◈

At home, a few days after the attack on their neighbors, Luncia saw her mother gathering the family valuables — silver candlesticks and bowls, gold necklaces and bracelets, and gilded picture frames.

"*Mamusia,* what are you doing?" Luncia asked.

"All Jewish families have been ordered to turn over their valuables to the Nazis," Barbara explained. "They say it's a contribution, but it's not. If they don't collect enough, they say they'll lock us in the synagogue and set it on fire. Come. Help me take these."

Together they carried the family valuables in a small sack to the synagogue and turned them over to the Nazis. Luncia glanced nervously at her mother's left hand. She winced when she saw that her mother had given up her wedding ring.

A short while later, a Gestapo officer barged into the Gamzers' apartment without knocking and barked, "Do you have any gold or silver?"

"Of course not," Barbara replied. "We gave it all as our *contribution.*" She said the last word in an almost mocking way. The officer glowered at Barbara, marched up to Luncia, and thrust his hands into the pockets of her dress. Startled, Luncia stood ramrod straight, too afraid to move, too terrified to ask what he was doing.

"Nothing in these pockets," he announced. "I know how clever you Jews can be. It's not unlike you to have hidden jewelry in your daughter's dress when you saw me coming." He sniffed the air. "Smells good. What are you cooking?"

Before Barbara could answer, he marched into the kitchen and pointed to the pot of potato soup simmering on the stove. "I want that pot."

"But I'm cooking in it," Barbara said.

"Not anymore." He poured the soup into the sink. "There. It's empty. Now wash the pot and give it to me." Luncia hated to see her mother reach for the pot because she knew there was nothing Barbara could do but follow the officer's orders.

As time passed, the days became increasingly grim for Luncia's family and the other Jews of Lvov. Luncia overheard her parents talking about how the Ukrainian nationalists, encouraged by the Nazis, began taking violent actions against the Jews and massacred 4,000 of them. A few weeks later, the nationalists kidnapped 2,000 Jews, forced them to march to the Jewish cemetery, and shot them. Fortunately for Luncia's family, none of the victims had been relatives.

Aktzia. The word alone brought terror. It meant the rounding up of Jews to be taken away and immediately shot or deported to concentration camps, where in most cases they were put to death. When an *aktzia* was called for,

Nazi officials issued to the Gestapo a quota — a required number — of Jews they had to capture. The Gestapo would sweep into a neighborhood and grab Jews right off the street. If they didn't catch enough, the Gestapo would storm into houses, apartment buildings, and stores, and drag Jews out until the quota was reached. Sometimes the *aktzia* targeted certain age groups of Jews, such as elderly people or children.

The Gamzers soon lost their store and had taken in another Jewish family, the Staubs — a husband and wife; their eight-year-old son, Henry; and his grandmother. The Staubs were among thousands in Lvov who had been permanently forced out of their homes by the Nazis. The two families now shared a one-bedroom apartment.

While playing with Henry one evening, Luncia noticed that her winter coat, which was trimmed in rabbit fur, was stretched across her mother's lap.

"What are you doing with my coat, *Mamusia*?" Luncia asked.

"We are collecting fur," Barbara replied. "It's needed for the German soldiers who are fighting in Russia. It will get very cold there soon." With a pair of scissors, she cut off all the coat's fur and did the same thing with Luncia's matching hat and muff. "I'm sorry, kitten. Jews aren't allowed to be seen with any fur."

Suddenly Luncia's father, Isaac, rushed into the apartment. "I just heard there's going to be another *aktzia*!" he cried frantically. "They're grabbing children. Quick, we must hide the kids!"

Barbara tossed a loaf of bread into a bag and filled two bottles with water. "Here, take this and hide in the bathroom," she told the two frightened children. "No matter what, do not make a peep. Not a whimper. And keep the light off. Understand?"

Luncia and Henry nodded and hurried into the darkened bathroom. Then the adults moved a large, beautifully carved wardrobe in front of the bathroom door. But the wardrobe wasn't tall enough to hide the door frame, so Barbara put a washtub and old suitcases on top to cover it. The adults hid all the children's clothes and any evidence that they even existed.

Luncia and Henry sat quietly in the dark, worrying about their safety in this deadly game of hide-and-seek. They were seized with fear when they heard a Ukrainian policeman and a Gestapo officer enter the apartment, looking for children.

"There are none here," said Isaac.

In the blackness of the bathroom, Luncia groped for Henry and squeezed him tight, a reminder to stay perfectly still. Barely breathing, Luncia listened to the conversation on the other side of the wardrobe.

The Gestapo officer pointed to a painting of Luncia hanging on the living room wall. The portrait had been made from a photo of her posing in a striped outfit when she was five. "This is your daughter, no?" the officer asked Isaac. "Where is she?"

My picture! thought Luncia. *We forgot all about it. How could we have been so careless to leave it up there?*

"Where is she?" the officer repeated, staring intently into Isaac's eyes.

Isaac replied, "They already took her away."

"It looks like you *used* to have a pretty child." The blunt statement was chillingly clear to the Gamzers. The Gestapo officer assumed that Luncia had met the same fate as other children caught in an earlier *aktzia* — death.

Meanwhile, the policeman stared at the wardrobe and peered at the space between its backside and the wall. He turned on his flashlight for a better look. When Luncia saw a sliver of light through the crack of the door, she was afraid the pounding of her heart would be loud enough to give them away. "Please, God, save us," she prayed silently over and over until her lips hurt.

At any moment, she was sure, the policeman would shout, "There's a secret room back here!" But he didn't.

When the two Nazis left, Isaac pushed the wardrobe aside and let Luncia and Henry out. "We were very lucky," said Isaac. "He must have seen the bathroom door. But for some reason he didn't give you away."

One morning, Grandma Staub entered the apartment and showed off her hair, which had been gray but was now dyed black. "So, what do you think?" she asked Barbara and Luncia.

"You look much younger," replied Barbara.

"Do you think I'll pass for forty?"

Barbara nodded, but not very convincingly.

Luncia looked quizzically at her mother, who whispered, "There's a rumor going around of an *aktzia* for older people only. That's why she wants to look younger."

Days later, Luncia wept when she learned that while walking down the street, Mrs. Staub had been taken away by the Gestapo, never to be seen again.

In early November, the Nazis ordered tens of thousands of Jews in Lvov to relocate to the city's north side, where they established an overcrowded Jewish ghetto. The Gamzers and their neighbors, the Holtzmans, a family of four, had to share one room of a tiny two-room house with no indoor plumbing. Two other families occupied the other room. They had just settled in when they heard shocking news — the Nazis had shot thousands of elderly and sick Jews as they crossed the bridge on Peltewna Street on their way to the ghetto.

Food and water were scarce in the ghetto, but somehow the Gamzers managed to scrounge up enough supplies to live — if facing death at any moment could be called living. No one ever knew when the Nazis would swoop into the ghetto and round up Jews for deportation, so under the porch of the house the four families dug a secret tunnel that led to a hiding place. At the first sign of the Nazis, the families would scurry into the hole, where they huddled in silence while the soldiers searched the house for them. The hideaway was barely big enough for one family, but somehow everyone in the house managed to squeeze into it.

Those were scary moments, during which each person

in the hiding place had to do absolutely nothing to give himself or herself away — no matter what the cost. And that was never more painfully true than the night the families were scrunched in the tiny space and heard familiar voices outside.

"Isaac, Isaac. Where are you? It's Hersh. I'm here with Bennie and Fannie."

"*Tatu*, it's Uncle Hersh and my cousins," Luncia murmured.

"Hush," whispered Isaac, clamping his hand over Luncia's mouth. "There's no more room. We can't even squeeze a flea in here. There's nothing we can do."

Luncia heard Hersh and his two children call out to them once more, pleading for help. And then . . . "Hurry, kids, the Nazis are coming!" Hersh said. In the hole, Luncia heard the three run off. Then she pressed her cheek against her father's chest, his big arms wrapped securely around her. She closed her eyes and prayed. And she felt her father's tears dripping onto her face.

A few days later, an old friend came to the house and told Luncia's family, "I have something awful to tell you. A Ukrainian policeman came to Hersh's room in the attic and demanded that he, Bennie, and Fannie come down to the courtyard. Hersh grabbed a knife from the table and said, 'If you don't leave, I'm going to stab you.' So the Ukrainian left, but he came back with the Gestapo. They took Hersh, Bennie, and Fannie away, and Grandma Sheindel, too. . . . And . . ."

"And what?" asked Isaac.

"They shot them all."

⊚   ⊚   ⊚

"Luncia," said her father a few nights later, "come sit on the couch with me. I have something important to tell you."

Luncia sat down, wondering if what her father wanted to discuss had to do with the way her parents had been whispering to each other over the past few days. "What is it, *Tatu*?" she asked.

"It is too dangerous for you to stay here in the ghetto. I've made arrangements for you to live with Mrs. Szczygiel."

Luncia gasped and began shaking her head. Isaac put a comforting hand on her thick brown hair.

"You know how much she likes you," he continued. "She has agreed to take you in and raise you like you're one of her daughters. But you won't be able to go outside. She's taking a big risk, because if the Nazis catch her hiding a Jew, she and her whole family will be executed."

Tears welled up in Luncia's eyes. "But I want to stay here with you and *Mamusia*."

"It's not safe here. This is your best chance, perhaps your only chance."

Yes, there was a big risk, he admitted. If Luncia was caught outside the ghetto, she would be shot. But there was no other choice. To stay meant almost certain death.

"How are you going to get me out of here?" she asked.

"I have a plan."

Isaac carried a special pass that allowed him to work in an office outside the ghetto because the Nazis considered him a "useful Jew."

Early the next morning, while it was still dark, Luncia kissed and hugged her mother good-bye, wondering if it would be the last time they'd ever see each other alive. Her father, who was wearing a long black overcoat, opened it up, and Luncia snuggled next to him, her left shoulder leaning against his right hip. Then he buttoned up his coat, hiding all of Luncia, except for her feet.

As they left the house, Isaac's coworker Mark, who also wore a long black overcoat, joined them. He walked shoulder to shoulder with Isaac so that Luncia was sandwiched between them under her father's coat.

I hope no one notices me, thought Luncia, as she tried to match the men's stride. With each passing minute, the tension grew inside her. *I wish we were there already. What if something goes wrong?*

Fortunately, everything went according to plan, and they soon reached the gate between the ghetto and the outside. They had to wait while another man ahead of them fumbled in his coat pocket looking for the pass that would allow him to leave.

"Hurry up!" shouted the impatient German guard.

"It's here somewhere. I know it is."

"You don't have a pass, do you?" snarled the guard. "You're trying to sneak out of the ghetto, trying to fool me."

"No, really, I have —" The man never finished his sentence. The guard shot him.

Hearing the loud bang, Luncia jerked. Her father wrapped his arms tight around his coat to keep her still, but her whole body trembled uncontrollably. *He's going to shoot us all, I know it. Oh, I wish we had never tried this.*

The guard rifled through the man's pocket and pulled out the pass. "He had a pass after all," he said to Isaac and Mark, who were still stunned from witnessing the senseless murder. "Too bad. The man had no luck." He motioned to the men. "Next."

Isaac and Mark whipped out their passes as Luncia held her breath and prayed. She continued to hold her breath even after the guard said, "Go on."

Once outside the ghetto, Isaac and Mark hustled Luncia into the nearby office building where they worked. She didn't stop shaking for hours.

Later that evening, her father had to leave the office. "Mrs. Szczygiel will be here in an hour, and she'll take you away," he said.

"When will I see you again?"

"As soon as the war is over, if not sooner."

They hugged. Luncia couldn't bring herself to let go. Finally, her father pried himself away, saying, "It's for the best. I love you, kitten. Be brave."

Luncia wanted to be brave, but she burst into tears. "What should I do now?" she sobbed.

"Just lie down on the desk and try to sleep."

Luncia remained there, scared and hungry and cold and worried. The hours ticked by and Mrs. Szczygiel failed to show up. By now, the rest of the Jewish workers had left the building, and Luncia was alone. She cried herself to sleep.

Isaac was shocked when he found Luncia slumped over his desk the next morning. Knowing Mrs. Szczygiel didn't have a phone, he sent a messenger, a sympathetic Christian teenager, to her house. The messenger reported back that the reason Mrs. Szczygiel hadn't come was that she had changed her mind.

"She got scared," the teenager reported. "She realized how dangerous it was for her. You know, it's death for people who hide Jews. But I told her that your daughter was waiting here all night, so the woman agreed to come. She'll be here this afternoon. She promised."

Mrs. Szczygiel finally arrived that afternoon and escorted Luncia out of the building. Luncia did not wear an armband with the Star of David, which the Nazis required of all Jews. She was posing as a non-Jew — an act punishable by death if she was caught. But she and Mrs. Szczygiel blended in with the bustle of the city. They took a streetcar to the woman's home, a narrow apartment that had a kitchen, a living room, a dining room, and a bedroom. The apartment was home to Mrs. Szczygiel; her husband, Boleshaw; their three teenage daughters, Yasha, Hella, and Marisia; and the girls' grandmother, who asked Luncia to call her *Babcia*.

Mr. and Mrs. Szczygiel slept in the living room, while

Luncia, *Babcia*, and the girls slept together in the bedroom.

Although *Babcia* didn't say much, she was kind to Luncia. But Luncia sensed right away that the teenage girls resented her, Luncia's, presence. She wasn't sure if it was because they didn't sympathize with her plight or because they blamed her for putting their lives in jeopardy. The girls seldom talked to her. She was told to sit in the corner of the living room in the burgundy love seat, not to go near the window or the door, and to hide under the bed behind the suitcases if anyone came to the apartment.

For the first few days, Luncia sobbed because she was so miserable, sitting there in the corner, no toy to play with, no book to read. She missed her parents terribly. Seeing her tears, Mrs. Szczygiel told Luncia, "You're lucky to be in my house, so stop your weeping." From then on, Luncia made sure no one ever saw her cry. She would sob into a hanky, and then dry it under the bed. While that one was drying, she would weep into her other hanky. After one particularly bad crying jag, she told herself, *Now I can't cry for a while because both hankies are wet. When they get dry, I can cry again.*

Luncia passed the time by telling herself tall tales, pretending that she was telling them to a bunch of children who were sitting at her feet. She made up happy stories of loving families going on exotic trips to far-off lands and meeting fascinating people.

She couldn't help but hear real children laughing and playing outside in the street. She pretended she was among them and made up stories about them, even matching names to their voices. *Those kids sound like they're having so much fun,* she thought to herself. *I wonder what they look like. Maybe I'll take a little peek out the window.* She moved to the window and peered outside, where she saw the children playing hopscotch. She smiled and daydreamed that one day she would be free to play like them.

Later that afternoon, Mrs. Szczygiel came home and scolded Luncia. "I told you never to go near the window! You could get this whole family killed!"

"I'm sorry. I didn't think anyone could see me."

"Well, the nosy neighbor across the street saw you and asked me who that little girl was. I said you were my niece. Luncia, everyone is suspicious of everyone. People are looking to turn in anyone who hides Jews so they can get money from the Nazis. The neighbors spy on one another. That's why you're strictly forbidden to go to the window. Just sit in the corner. Do you promise?"

Luncia nodded and slumped in the chair. "I just wanted a peek."

What Luncia really wanted was for Mrs. Szczygiel and the family to give her a little warmth, a friendly hug, a comforting word. Luncia had always been showered with love by her parents. But just to be treated with the same amount of affection the Szczygiels showed Jockey, the family Chihuahua, would have been good enough for her then. The Szczygiel family *did* care about her, Luncia reasoned — after all, they were risking their lives to hide her. Still, she thought, they had a weird way of showing their feelings toward her.

"Here, put this on," said Mrs. Szczygiel one day, holding up Luncia's treasured spring coat. It had big blue checks and a matching hat.

Luncia's eyes lit up. "Are we going outside?"

"No. I need to sell some things so we'll have money to buy food from the farmers. I figure that since you can't go outside anyway, there's no reason for you to have this pretty coat. It should bring us a nice price. But before I sell it, I want you to wear it one last time."

And so Luncia did. She closed her eyes and pictured herself walking in the autumn forest, leaves of gold and crimson tickling her face as they fluttered to the ground. Then she opened her eyes and slowly took off the coat. "Thank you," she said.

Luncia understood this gesture was Mrs. Szczygiel's way — no matter how awkward it was — of being thoughtful. It wasn't quite as considerate, or as dangerous, as the time when Mr. Szczygiel led Luncia by the hand and opened the front door so she could get a glimpse of children singing Christmas carols. Luncia knew he had taken a grave risk, and she was forever grateful to him for that brief moment of joy.

Happy moments were rare for Luncia during her long, boring days of hiding, so when she learned from the Szczygiels that her parents had sneaked out of the ghetto, she buzzed with delight. (Their escape was crucial, because the Nazis were deporting 65,000 Jews from the ghetto to the Belzec death camp.) Isaac and Barbara had made it safely to the home of their former employees, the Ojaks, who were Christian. Luncia pictured what life must be like for her parents hiding at the Ojaks. She giggled, imagining grouchy Mr. Ojak swatting her mother's hand away as she tried to lick frosting off one of his bowls.

Luncia's imagination was her only escape from the day-to-day boredom — that, and taking cover whenever visitors arrived.

When the landlord decided to paint the apartment, Mr. Szczygiel had to stuff Luncia into a burlap sack and carry her into the cellar so the painters wouldn't see her. After putting wood chips over her, he left her in the sack all day and brought her up at night to eat and sleep. For three days, from morning until evening, she had to remain in that sack, because residents of the apartment building often entered the cellar.

Despite all the precautions, more than once, Luncia was seen — and only the quick thinking of Mrs. Szczygiel saved Luncia from being turned over to the Nazis.

One day, Luncia was left alone in the apartment. She had been told not to let anyone in unless she heard a special knock. That afternoon, someone knocked at the door. Thinking it was Mrs. Szczygiel, Luncia opened the door. To her shock, she stood face-to-face with a man in uniform.

Luncia panicked. She ran into the bedroom, slammed the door, and hid under the bed, while the man kept calling, "Hey, come back here."

She shivered in fear, expecting the man to enter the

bedroom at any second and drag her away. But then she heard the front door slam shut.

When Mrs. Szczygiel came home later, a neighbor across the hall told her that the mailman said a crazy little girl had opened the door and run away. He wanted to investigate but wouldn't search the apartment alone. So he asked the neighbor to go in with him, but by then the wind had blown the door shut.

The next day, Mrs. Szczygiel told the mailman the same thing she had told the neighbor: "I'm so sorry about what happened. My niece from Krakow is visiting, and she's a wild kid. I don't know why she acted that way, she's very unpredictable."

Everyone in the family was upset, especially Hella and Marisia. Luncia understood why. Hella was dating Filip, a young man who had links to the Nazi-supporting Ukrainian secret police. To find a Jew would be a big feather in his cap — and spell doom for the Szczygiels and for Luncia.

Luncia managed to stay hidden from Filip whenever he came over. But one evening, while Luncia was sitting by the Christmas tree, which was lit with candles, he unexpectedly showed up.

Filip spotted Luncia. But because the room was so dim, he thought she was Marisia and said, "Merry Christmas, Marisia. How are you?"

Filled with panic, Luncia struggled for breath. *I don't know what to do. I can't run. Should I pretend I'm Marisia? I should do something before he gets suspicious. But what?*

Realizing Filip had mistaken Luncia for Marisia, Mrs. Szczygiel told him, "Oh, that Marisia. She had an argument with me today and now she's pouting. Never mind her."

In an incredible stroke of luck, Marisia was in the bathroom at the time. So Mrs. Szczygiel whisked Luncia out of the room and hid her, then whispered to Marisia what had happened.

Weeks later, Luncia was bringing a tray of food to Marisia, who was sick in bed with the flu, when Marisia's boyfriend, Tomasz, appeared at the front door without warning. Luncia had just enough time to slip under the bed and hide behind the suitcases.

Tomasz, who also supported the Nazis, came into the room and pulled up a chair next to the bed to chat with Marisia. Jockey trotted in right behind him. The dog sniffed Luncia's scent and began growling and yelping, pawing at the floor under the bed.

Oh, no! I'm going to get caught because of that stupid dog! Luncia thought, angrily waving her hand at Jockey, hoping he'd go away.

"What's the matter, Jockey?" Tomasz asked. "What do you see under there?"

Luncia broke out in a sweat. *This is it. It's all over for me.*

Tomasz got off the chair and kneeled down, but before he could look under the bed, Marisia grabbed his arm and said, "Oh, Tomasz, it's nothing. How about giving me a hug to make me feel better?"

"Of course, my dumpling."

So that Jockey wouldn't give Luncia's hiding spot away again, Marisia called the dog up onto the bed and held him during Tomasz's visit. When he left, Marisia burst into tears of relief after the close call. So did Luncia.

That evening, as she lay in bed, Luncia overheard the family talking about her. The girls were afraid that it was only a matter of time before Luncia was discovered. "We don't want her in the house anymore," declared Marisia. "It's too dangerous for all of us."

"I'm sad to say I think the girls are right," Mr. Szczygiel said.

"So what are we going to do with her?" asked Mrs. Szczygiel. "We can't just throw her out in the street. How would she survive? Besides, if we do, the police will catch her, and then they'll torture her until she tells them about us."

"We'll have to do something," her husband said. "One more slipup, and we could all die."

The next day, with *Babcia*'s help, Mrs. Szczygiel decided to hide Luncia from her husband and girls — but still in the house. Pointing to a wooden trunk under the window in the kitchen, Mrs. Szczygiel told Luncia, "That's your new hiding spot until I find a safe house for you." *Babcia* cut out holes for air and then made Luncia get into the trunk and closed the lid. Although Luncia was short and skinny, the trunk was still too small for her body. The only way she could fit in it was to lie curled up in a ball. She was allowed to get out during the day when the girls and Mr. Szczygiel were at school or work. But before they got home, she had to climb back into the trunk. To explain her absence, Mrs. Szczygiel told the rest of the family that she had found a new home for Luncia.

The problem with this scheme was Jockey. He would sniff around the trunk when Luncia was hiding inside, making the girls think there was a mouse in the kitchen. One morning, when Marisia went to the kitchen window to see if it was raining, Luncia was hiding in the trunk, trying to twist her body into a more comfortable position. Marisia heard the noise and, thinking it was the mouse, grabbed a broom and opened the trunk. Much to her surprise, instead of finding a rodent, she discovered Luncia. The truth was out . . . and the rest of the family wasn't pleased.

The next morning, Mrs. Szczygiel told Luncia, "Get ready. I'm taking you to see the Ojaks."

Knowing that meant she would be seeing her parents for the first time in eight months, Luncia wanted to let out a joyous yell. But because she so seldom spoke, it came out sounding more like a squeak. "Oh, that's the best news ever!" she managed to say. The thrilled girl couldn't wait to cuddle in the arms of her mother and father after being apart from them for so long.

But sitting constantly during her stay had taken a physical toll on Luncia. Mrs. Szczygiel and *Babcia* had to help her exercise her leg muscles because they were so weak from going unused. She even had to practice how to speak clearly again after months of barely saying anything.

That afternoon, Luncia again posed as a non-Jew in

public, knowing that if she was caught, she'd be shot. But when she stepped outside for the first time since November, she forgot her fears. As she basked in the warmth of the July sunshine, her eyes hungrily took in all the activity around her — trucks, autos, and streetcars whizzing by, children playing soccer in the streets, and the flowers blooming in bursts of vibrant color.

She and Mrs. Szczygiel climbed onto a streetcar and headed for the Ojaks' home. Luncia's mind whirled with mixed emotions. She was so eager to see her parents again and was excited to be a part of city life, but she was scared of being discovered.

About a mile before their stop, Mrs. Szczygiel suddenly grabbed Luncia and took her off the streetcar. "We'll walk the rest of the way," she told her.

"Why?"

"I didn't like the way one of the passengers was staring at you."

With each block, as Luncia soaked in the sights and smells of the city, her fear faded and her excitement grew. It reached its peak when they arrived at the Ojaks' home.

Mr. Ojak, displaying his usual sour expression, answered the door, stared at Luncia and Mrs. Szczygiel, and scowled. "What's going on?"

Mrs. Szczygiel shoved Luncia forward and told him, "We can't keep her any longer. You have to take her."

It was clear to Luncia that Mr. Ojak had no clue they were coming and was unprepared to take her in. He frowned and rubbed his chin. After several awkward seconds of silence, he motioned them into the house, saying, "She can stay. If I'm caught, it's the same death for me whether I'm hiding two Jews or three."

Before Mr. Ojak finished his sentence, Luncia spotted her parents in the room, dashed past him, and jumped into their arms. She peppered her mother and father with tearful, happy kisses and was smothered in warm hugs in return. Then Luncia gushed to her parents, "The world is so beautiful, and I'd like so much to live."

"You will, kitten," promised her father. "You will."

At this, everyone in the room started crying — even crabby old Mr. Ojak.

◎

Luncia and her parents hid with the Ojaks for a year, until liberation in May 1945. The Gamzers then lived for a short time in Munich, Germany, before coming to the United States in 1949 and settling in Brooklyn, New York. Luncia decided to change her name to Ruth, which sounded more American. In the States, she went to school and started living the life of a typical teenager.

In New York, Ruth began dating Jack Gruener, a Holocaust survivor she had met in Munich. (His story appears later in this book.) The couple married in 1953, built a successful interior-design company, and raised two sons, who gave them four grandchildren. Ruth is a volunteer at the Museum of Jewish Heritage in New York City, where she tells her story to children visiting the museum. She and Jack also visit schools throughout the city to talk about the Holocaust.

Ruth is the little girl in the photo on the cover of this book. It was taken when she was five years old. Her parents had a portrait made from that photo, and it was that painting that caught the Nazi's eye when Ruth was

hiding in the bathroom. After the Gamzers moved to the ghetto, Ruth's fa-
ther put the family's cherished photographs — including the one of Ruth —
into a jar and buried it for safekeeping. When the war ended, he returned to
the ghetto and found the jar. The photos were still inside, safe and sound,
for the family to treasure.

Herbert Karliner was excited. The twelve-year-old and his entire family were walking up the gangplank of a luxury steamship that would take them away from all the heartache and misery of a homeland that had rejected them.

Herbert, his three siblings, and his parents were among the 937 Jews who were boarding the S.S. *St. Louis* in Hamburg, Germany, on a balmy spring day in 1939. They were bound for what they hoped was a new life in Cuba and eventually the United States. Although the children were looking forward to this new adventure, Herbert could tell his parents were sad. They had been forced to leave Germany . . . or face death.

As he reached the main deck, Herbert clutched his

passport, certain it was a permit that finally would free him from terror. Unfortunately, it would turn out that he was holding a passport to nowhere — and only further hardships lay ahead.

◎　　◎　　◎

The first hint of trouble back home had come on the soccer field. Herbert loved soccer and was one of the best center forwards in all of Peiskretscham, Germany. His classmates marveled at the way he could weave downfield so cleverly that he'd leave defenders sprawled on the ground. Almost every day after school, Herbert would play soccer with his friends. But in 1938, shortly before he turned twelve, he began to notice that instead of going after the ball, the defenders were elbowing him hard in the ribs, knocking him down, and deliberately kicking him in the shins.

Herbert would limp home, bruised and bleeding. Sometimes on the way, he'd get attacked by older kids, who would leap out of the bushes, shove him to the side-walk, and then run off. Other times, he'd find himself surrounded by boys who would taunt him and curse at him — simply because he was Jewish. There weren't many Jews in the town of 15,000 — only about 80 families. They were increasingly becoming targets of townspeople who were encouraged by their country's leader, Adolf Hitler, to spread anti-Semitism.

Even Herbert's closest friends — two non-Jewish brothers — turned on him and began calling him a "dirty

Jew." When Herbert's father, Joseph, learned what had happened, he took Herbert and confronted the boys' dad, who was a friend of the family.

"My boy didn't do anything wrong," Herbert's father told the friend. "Tell your sons to leave him alone."

The friend replied, "I'm sorry, Joseph, but I can't do anything. If I try to stop them, other people will give me hell, and then the police will come and pick me up."

Herbert knew how true that was. His uncle Paul had made a critical remark about Hitler that someone overheard, and the next day he was taken to a concentration camp in Dachau, Germany. A few weeks later, an SS officer showed up at the door of Herbert's aunt, handed her a small box, and said, "Here, you can have your husband back." Inside were his ashes.

The harassment of Jews in Peiskretscham became so intense that Herbert had to give up attending school, playing soccer, and going to the movies. He could hardly even walk along the quiet streets of the town where he had always felt safe and had played with his friends. Now these children were no longer his friends. And he no longer felt safe, especially after *Kristallnacht* — the Night of Broken Glass.

On the evenings of November 9 and 10, 1938, rampaging Nazi-backed mobs throughout Germany and Austria attacked Jews in the street, in their homes, and at their places of work and worship. At least 96 Jews were killed and hundreds more injured, more than 1,000 synagogues were burned, hundreds of Jewish cemeteries and schools were damaged, and almost 7,500 Jewish businesses were vandalized and looted — including the Karliners' grocery store.

Herbert; his fourteen-year-old brother, Walter; his sixteen-year-old sister, Ilse; his eleven-year-old sister, Ruth; and their parents, Joseph and Martha, were asleep in the living quarters in the back of the store when the mob shattered the windows in the front, facing the street. The invaders swarmed into the shop, pulled boxes and cans of food off the shelves, smashed them on the floor, and squashed all the fresh fruit and vegetables before running off to destroy another store.

As the stunned family surveyed the damage, a Jewish friend rushed in and shouted, "The synagogue is burning!"

The Karliners raced down the street to the synagogue, where flames were shooting out of the broken windows. In front, Nazis were laughing and cheering at the bonfire they had made out of the prayer books they had seized from the synagogue. The Jews on the street dropped to their knees, crying and begging for them to stop. The wailing grew louder when the Nazis grabbed the sacred Torah scroll and tossed it into the fire.

Joseph could stand it no longer. He shoved aside the Nazis and tried to retrieve the Torah, but they grabbed him and beat him, keeping him down until the scroll had turned to ash. Then they left him, bleeding, facedown in the street.

Herbert and his brother rushed to their father's aid. As they helped him to his feet, a Nazi sneered at them and hissed, "The Gestapo will come soon and take all of you away."

Later that night, the Gestapo stormed into the Karliners' ruined store and dragged Herbert's father away, leaving the rest of the family fearing for his life. They soon learned he had been sent to Buchenwald, one of Germany's largest concentration camps. During this time, the Nazis were willing to release certain prisoners, but only after they had purchased a special permit that allowed them to leave the country for good. Martha managed to scrape together enough money to obtain the proper documents for Joseph's release. But it meant that Joseph would have to move to China, which was accepting a small number of Jews.

After Joseph was freed, however, he learned that the Cuban Consul in Hamburg, Germany, was selling permits to go to Cuba, where several of his relatives had fled months earlier. He purchased permits and passage for himself and his entire family. That meant selling virtually everything they owned, and at a huge loss. The Gestapo forced Joseph to sell his store and home, worth $100,000 at the time, for only $10,000. To further strangle the family financially, the Gestapo refused to let them take most of their own money out of Germany. And anything they bought for the trip was taxed at a rate of 100 percent, which meant that whatever they bought had to be purchased at double the price.

The Karliners had little choice. At least they would be free of the terror the Nazis had unleashed against the Jews, or so they believed. The family hoped that by going to Cuba they could eventually get to the United States, even though it might take years. The problem was that by law, the U.S. could accept no more than 26,000 German immigrants a year. Unfortunately, in 1939, there were six times that many who, like the Karliners, had applied for visas to enter the States.

Herbert and his siblings had always wanted to go to America. Herbert had read books and magazines about this exciting country where buildings soared into the sky, cowboys roamed the West, and families drove fancy new cars. It was the country that cheered for a black athlete named Jesse Owens, who had won four gold medals at the 1936 Olympic Games in Berlin, upsetting Hitler so much that the dictator refused to shake his hand.

On Saturday, May 13, 1939, Herbert was one of the 937 passengers, all Jewish refugees, who boarded the black-and-white ocean liner at pier 76 in Hamburg, Germany. At 8 P.M., the ship, flying under a Nazi flag, set sail. Some passengers wept from relief at finally escaping Hitler's terror; others wept from sadness at the thought that they might never again see the loved ones they had left behind. The younger passengers, like Herbert, were just thrilled to begin a new adventure.

No one imagined they were on a voyage of the doomed.

On board, families began to relax and enjoy the food, the movies, and the dancing. On orders from the ship's captain, Gustav Schroeder, the German crew was to treat the passengers with kindness and respect. The crew even took down the picture of Adolf Hitler in the ballroom when the passengers held their religious services there. (The picture was promptly put back up when the services ended.)

During the two-week crossing of the Atlantic, Herbert had a wonderful time. He enjoyed swimming in the pool, making new friends, and joining in silly pranks like soaping doorknobs and locking bathroom stall doors, then crawling out underneath.

Before daybreak on May 27, Herbert eagerly woke up and raced onto the deck so he could watch the *St. Louis* steam into Cuba's Havana harbor. *So this is going to be my new home*, he thought, gazing through the early morning light at a city that was starting to stir. *I can't wait to get off.* He scanned the docks, hoping to spot his cousins, who had been in Cuba for a couple of months. But he couldn't find them.

By the time he returned to the cabin, the Karliners had all their suitcases packed and ready outside the door. Showing off his Spanish to his family, Herbert said, *"Buenas dias. Como esta usted?"* ("Good morning. How are you?")

His brother and sisters laughed, but Herbert could tell his parents were not in the best frame of mind. They were uneasy because they had to start a new life with no money in a new country, and they had to learn a new language. Despite their worries, they were thankful they were no longer subject to Hitler's cruelty.

Once the *St. Louis* docked, the refugees were filled with happy anticipation and couldn't wait to step onto Cuban soil. However, by late in the day, only twenty-two people had been allowed off the ship. The rest had to stay on board.

"What's wrong, Papa?" Herbert asked. "We've been waiting for hours. When do we get off?"

"I don't know," Joseph replied. "They say there's some difficulty with the passengers' permits. They keep saying, 'Wait, wait.'"

What the refugees didn't know was that ten days before the ship sailed out of Hamburg, the Cuban president, Federico Laredo Bru, had changed his nation's immigration rules. The steamship official responsible for immigration documents hadn't told the passengers, believing that their documents to enter Cuba were in order because they were dated before the new rules went into effect. The official was mistaken. President Laredo Bru refused to honor the permits, so an international committee for refugees tried to convince him to change his mind. The president was willing, but for a price — $500 per passenger. Unfortunately, no one carried that kind of money because the Nazis hadn't let the passengers take that much out of Germany.

The talks between the committee and the Cuban president dragged on for days, changing the mood on board from excitement to boredom, from hope to despair. Passengers crowded the ship's radio room and sent hundreds of telegrams to important people like President Franklin D. Roosevelt, other American politicians, Jewish leaders, and heads of international organizations, begging for help. First Lady Eleanor Roosevelt was asked to at least save the children of the *St. Louis*. Telegrams were wired to Europe, South America, Central America, and the United States. The response left the refugees depressed. Most people didn't reply to the telegrams or, if they did, said there was nothing they could do.

Meanwhile, relatives already living in Cuba rowed out in small boats and surrounded the *St. Louis*. For five days they shouted encouragement and news to the refugees, who pressed against the rails on the deck high above or stuck their heads out of the portholes.

Two of Herbert's cousins rowed out and yelled to the Karliners to have faith. "We're trying our best to get you off the ship. We're working with the Cuban government and the Jewish community."

While the ship remained at anchor, Cuban police patrolled the docks to restrain a mob of Nazi sympathizers that had formed to jeer at the families and friends gathered in support of the refugees. The mob was the result of a devious scheme plotted back in Germany by Joseph Goebbels, head of Nazi propaganda. One of Goebbels's tactics was to spread false information in order to sway public opinion. He had sent agents to Havana to stir up anti-Semitism by telling the Cuban people that most of the passengers were criminals, which made them undesirable. The agents organized protests against allowing the "Jewish criminals" to enter Cuba.

Herbert could feel the tension on board increasing day by day. He heard passengers saying that if they were forced back to Germany, they would surely be sent to concentration camps. One man couldn't take the strain anymore and leaped overboard, but he was rescued. Concerned that more refugees would jump ship, the Cuban government increased the number of police boats patrolling the water and trained spotlights on the ship at night.

On Friday morning, June 2, the Cuban government informed Captain Schroeder that if the ship didn't leave peacefully, the navy would force it to leave. So the *St. Louis* started its engines and slowly moved out. Herbert was on deck, his eyes misting up as weeping passengers shouted their farewells to friends and family in the rented boats below.

"Papa, what's going to happen to us?" Herbert asked.

"I don't know," his father replied. "Let us hope that some country will take us. If we are forced to go back to Germany . . ." Joseph didn't finish his sentence. But Herbert understood. They faced almost certain death.

Captain Schroeder tried to delay the return to Germany by guiding his ship slowly along the southeastern coast of Florida, hoping that a new flurry of telegrams would finally convince a friendly country to accept the refugees. Herbert hung around the ship's bustling radio room, getting the latest news: "The Dominican Republic will let us in . . ." "An island off Cuba is going to take us . . ." "A rich American who owns an island off New Orleans has agreed to let us stay there." Every promising report brought cheers, but each report turned out to be false, crushing the hopes of the refugees.

The ship sailed to within a mile of Miami Beach, so close that Herbert could see palm trees swaying in the breeze and pastel-colored hotels dotting the shoreline. The beach seemed so close, so achingly close, that Herbert wanted to leap into the water and swim to shore. If he were bigger and bolder, he just might have done it. *If only I could . . .* He imagined himself playing soccer on the beach and drinking coconut milk and diving for seashells. And being free. *Someday, I'm going to come back here,* he told himself. *Someday, I will make this place my home.*

By Tuesday, June 6, time had run out. With supplies of food and water shrinking, Captain Schroeder reluctantly ordered the ship to set a course back to Germany — a decision that left hundreds of refugees crying in anguish. *Is there no country in the entire world that will take us?* Herbert wondered. *We're good people. What's wrong with us? No, what's wrong with the rest of the world?* He tried not to think about it, but it was hard not to. All he had to do was look at the cheerless faces of the adults to feel the gloom that had washed over the ship. Every Jew on board felt alone and rejected by the world.

Back in Germany, Goebbels used the plight of the *St. Louis* passengers to further his anti-Semitic propaganda when, during a speech to the nation, he said, "You see? Nobody wants the Jews."

During the crossing, Herbert overheard a group of German Jews who, months earlier, had been imprisoned with his father. They were plotting a mutiny. "We're never going to go back to Buchenwald," the leader pledged.

"We'll take over the ship. Does anyone know how to run a ship?" It didn't matter whether anyone did or didn't. They had to do something.

Captain Schroeder eased tensions by telling them, "I will not return you to Germany. If I must, I'll put everyone in lifeboats and scuttle [deliberately sink] the ship off the coast of England. Under international law, they must come and rescue us, and then you'll be on British soil."

But such a drastic measure wasn't necessary. At the last moment, four countries — Holland, Belgium, France, and England — each agreed to accept about 200 passengers from the *St. Louis*.

"Our lives have been spared!" shouted Herbert's father. The passengers danced and laughed and cried with relief. Once again, the mood on board was happy, and it remained that way when the ship docked in Antwerp, Belgium, on June 20, ending an emotional thirty-eight-day journey. But for Herbert and his family and the rest of the refugees, the ordeal was really just beginning.

Friends and relatives were split up. Some were shipped to England, others to France or Holland. The rest were allowed to stay in Belgium.

The Karliners were sent to France. Because Joseph and Martha had no money and no job, they left Herbert and Walter at a children's home outside of Paris. The parents and their daughters, Ilse and Ruth, were taken to Mirambeau, a small village near the central Atlantic coast, where they posed as French citizens.

Ten weeks later, on September 1, Germany invaded

Poland, triggering the start of World War II. In a heartbreaking turn of events, three of the four countries in which the *St. Louis* refugees had settled would soon fall under the control of the Nazis.

In the spring of 1940, Germany attacked France. For the Karliner brothers' safety, they were transferred 185 miles (nearly 300 kilometers) south to the Chaumont Children's Home in Creuse, where they blended in with the rest of the kids, who were mostly non-Jews.

In early summer, France surrendered to Germany, and the country was divided into two zones — occupied and unoccupied. The Nazis controlled the occupied zone of northern and western France and the entire Atlantic coast, including Mirambeau. The unoccupied zone in the southern half was ruled by a French government operating in the city of Vichy. The Vichy government cooperated with the Nazis and promised to hand over to the Nazis all the Jews in France. It also agreed to pay the occupation costs of the German troops and to prevent any French people from leaving the country.

The Chaumont Children's Home was in the unoccupied zone. Because the home was short on money, the older boys had to go to work to replace the men in the village who had been taken away by the army. Walter worked for a cabinetmaker. Herbert, who was now almost fourteen, became a baker. For the next two and a half years, he had to get up at 3 A.M., walk nearly two miles (three kilometers) to the bakery, work for several hours, then return to the home for schooling.

After working nearly every day for a year in the bakery, Herbert was given a week's vacation. He missed his family terribly, so he decided to visit his parents and sisters in Mirambeau, about 150 miles (240 kilometers) away in the occupied zone.

Without permission or the necessary documents, Herbert left Creuse and, by hitchhiking and taking a train and a bus, reached the border between the two zones. With the help of a map, he sneaked across the border into German-occupied territory. He knew he had to be careful, because if the Nazis caught him, he would be sent to a concentration camp. After sleeping in the woods at night, he walked another eighteen miles (twenty-nine kilometers) to the home where his parents and sisters were living. The family shared a heartwarming, tearful reunion that made the difficulty of Herbert's journey feel worthwhile.

When it was time for Herbert to return, his father told him, "After the war is over and the Nazis are defeated, make sure you come back here to Mirambeau. We'll meet you here, and then life will be good again."

His mother stuffed some money into Herbert's pocket and said, "Promise me you won't sleep in the woods. Once you cross the border, stop at the first hotel you see and spend the night there."

"I promise, Mama."

Herbert avoided the Nazi soldiers in the occupied zone and sneaked back across the border, arriving at a hotel at about 11 P.M. "I'd like a room, please," he said.

The clerk replied, "Let me see your papers first."

"I don't have any. I'm from the children's home in Creuse."

The clerk studied Herbert, who didn't fit the stereotypical Jewish profile because he had blond hair and blue eyes. Somewhat reluctantly, the clerk handed Herbert a room key. In the room, Herbert immediately plopped down on the bed and fell asleep, dreaming about basking in the sun in Miami Beach. But at 3 A.M., a loud pounding on the door jarred him awake. "Police! Open up!"

Unable to show the police any papers, Herbert was hustled off to jail, where he was peppered with questions: *Where did you come from? Where were you going? Why don't you have papers? What are you doing in this village?*

Herbert didn't dare tell the officers anything about visiting his parents. In fact, he said as little as possible other than that he had come from the children's home in Creuse. After the police checked his story out, they let him go. When he returned to Creuse, he was scolded by officials, taken to court, and fined for leaving the home without proper documents.

Herbert knew he needed to be more careful. It was a dangerous world, and one wrong move could spell disaster.

In the children's home, the older kids had to look after the younger ones. At night, the teens took turns standing watch in case the Nazi-backed police showed up, searching for Jews. All the Jewish children slept in their clothes and had, within reach, a bag of sugar and bread for those frightening times when they had to flee into the woods.

Among the kids Herbert looked after was a boy named Kurt Birk, who suffered from asthma. One night, when they were awakened by a warning that the police were arriving, Herbert and the other Jewish kids scurried into the woods. Kurt was very sick and weak, so Herbert and his brother, Walter, carried him. Unfortunately, Kurt's tension and anxiety from the escape triggered an asthma attack, and Kurt started coughing and wheezing. Fearing that Kurt would give away their location, Herbert pulled out a handkerchief and shoved it into Kurt's mouth, keeping him quiet until the police went away.

The potential danger from these raids kept mounting. On a summer night in 1942, Herbert was sleeping in the bakery when the police barged in with guns drawn. They took him away to a camp where older teenage boys, including many from the children's home, were being held. The authorities announced that anybody sixteen and older would be sent to a forced-labor camp, while the younger ones would be released because they were considered too young yet for slave work. Herbert was let go, but it was a close call — he was just one week away from turning sixteen.

Fortunately, Walter had escaped the raid and, with the help of the French underground, found a safe haven elsewhere.

It was clear that Herbert couldn't stay at the children's home. The police would no doubt return soon, and when they did, he would be old enough for deportation like the older boys, who were never seen again. The French underground gave Herbert forged documents and a new identity — he became a French citizen named Paul Brun. He and another Jewish boy, who also had a false French ID, headed toward Spain on a train.

At a railroad checkpoint, the Gestapo entered the train and looked at the travel documents of all the passengers. Herbert *had* to act calm. If he showed any sign of nervousness, the Gestapo could become suspicious. As they walked down the aisle, the officers began questioning two teenagers who, Herbert knew, were Jews trying to pass themselves off as French citizens. But the boys were too jittery and unsure when they answered the Gestapo's stern questions. Suddenly, the Gestapo — unhappy with the answers — dragged the boys off the train.

Now those same officers confronted Herbert and his friend. *Stay calm,* Herbert told himself. *Look them in the eye. Act like you're not afraid of them.* Outwardly he appeared cool, but inside he was a bundle of nerves. He hoped his eyes wouldn't betray how scared he was as he handed the Gestapo his fake documents.

The officers examined Herbert's travel papers closely and studied his mannerisms. Herbert could only hope that his blue eyes and blond hair would make them less suspicious of him. The policemen grunted and handed the papers back to Herbert and his friend before moving on.

When the two teenagers reached the Spanish border, a French pastor met them and told them, "I don't think it's a good idea to go to Spain. They are turning refugees away, but they're not shipping them back. They're turning them over to the Nazis."

Eventually, the French underground managed to put Herbert to work as a farmhand in Treves-Rhone, France, where he posed as a French Catholic and even went to Mass every Sunday with the owner of the farm. Being a farmhand was grueling work, but at least Herbert had a roof over his head and fresh food in his stomach. He wrote to his parents often, but always in a way that wouldn't give anyone reading his letters — like the Gestapo — an idea that they were Jews.

In the fall of 1942, Herbert started to worry because he hadn't received any letters from his parents for many weeks. With each unanswered letter, his heart ached a little bit more. He kept remembering what his father had told him, that after the war, the whole family would be reunited "and then life will be good again."

Herbert tried not to think the worst and focused on his other concerns — like keeping his true identity secret.

One day, while Herbert was working on the farm, a policeman with graying hair showed up and asked to see his papers. By now, Herbert felt confident in dealing with these tense situations and calmly handed over the fake documents.

"Ah, I see you are from Cernay," the officer said.

"Yes," said Herbert. "From the Alsace region near the German border."

"I know it well. I was there during the First World War."

Suddenly, Herbert felt his stomach twist in a knot. *What am I going to do? I've never been to that town. What if he quizzes me? One wrong answer, and I could end up in a concentration camp.* His whole body began to shake, so to cover up the trembling he coughed. *You must stay calm!* he told himself firmly.

"It was a fierce battle there," said the aging officer. "Many killed. I understand the bones of twelve thousand soldiers are in the town crypt, right?"

How should I answer? If I'm wrong, I'm in deep trouble. Just agree with him. "Yeah, right. The crypt."

"The old trenches and war shelters, are they still there?"

Herbert nodded. *Get him to talk so he won't ask any more questions.* "Were you injured during the battle?" Herbert asked.

"No, by the grace of God I was not." The officer then rattled off a couple of war stories, and Herbert began to relax. *No more questions, please.*

"So — and this is a very important question, young man — is that tavern still there, the one with the big curved door near the statue?" the officer asked.

Is this a trick question? Is he trying to trip me up? However you answer, say it with certainty. "Yeah, and it serves the best beer in all of Alsace," Herbert said at last.

The officer gave a hearty laugh and handed the documents back to Herbert. "I must go back there sometime, maybe when this war is over."

"I hope to see you there."

After the policeman left, it took nearly an hour before Herbert could stop trembling.

In the fall of 1944, Herbert ran away from the farm and went to Paris, which by then had been liberated by the Americans. There he found his brother, Walter. Herbert joined an organization that helped reunite relatives with many of the thousands of Jewish children who had concealed their identities by living with — and as — Christians. Because he could speak German, French, and Yiddish, Herbert soon was traveling throughout France to assist these hidden children.

Although Herbert had much success with his mission, he yearned for one special reunion — the one with his own family. After the war, Herbert returned to Mirambeau just as he had promised his parents he would do. The words of his father — "and then life will be good again" — still echoed in his mind from the last time he had seen him four years earlier. Herbert wanted so much to believe that the family would return together to Germany. He dreamed that the store and the apartment in back would once again be as they were before *Kristallnacht* — filled with the love and laughter of his mother and father and sisters. But it was not to be.

Herbert learned that Joseph and Martha and Ilse and Ruth would never be coming back. They had been captured by the Gestapo in the fall of 1942 and deported to Auschwitz, a notorious death camp in Poland, where they — like an estimated 1 million other victims — were killed.

Despite his overwhelming heartache, Herbert was determined to make something of himself. After the agony of the *St. Louis* and so many years of hiding, he decided to find a place where he could once again believe that life could truly be good. He knew it was what his family would have wanted for him.

◎

Herbert and his brother, Walter, arrived in the United States on December 29, 1946. Herbert lived in Hartford, Connecticut, where he went to night school and worked as a baker. After he served two years in the United States Army, Herbert's boyhood dream came true. In 1952, he moved to Miami Beach — which he calls "paradise" — and he has been there ever since. Herbert and his wife, Vera, a Holocaust survivor who also hid in France, raised two daughters and now have three grandchildren.

Walter, who never married, became a dentist and lives in Westbrook, Connecticut, where he owns an antique shop.

Of the 937 passengers aboard the St. Louis, *it is estimated that about half died in concentration camps.*

So This Is Where I'm Going to Die
Markus Reich's Story

One step at a time, Markus Reich told himself. *Just one step at a time.*

The bitter cold and icy wind lashed at Markus's red-dened, cracked skin as he and his buddy Stefan Schreiber trudged through the snow. On their weary shoulders they carried a heavy ten-foot-long (three-meter-long) piece of lumber.

"You know, we'll be killed for this," said Stefan, who was leading the way. "If the Nazis don't shoot us, we'll die from the cold."

"No, this will work," said Markus. "It must work. . . ." His voice trailed off. It hurt to talk because the blast of wind stung his teeth and gums whenever he opened his mouth. "No matter what, stick with the plan. We will fool the Nazi guards . . . or die trying."

It was a daring plan. Two Jewish seventeen-year-olds, pretending to be regular Polish workers, had just walked out of a Nazi slave-labor camp. Now all they had to do was keep slogging through the snow for days and days to reach their hometown — and they had to do it in the dead of winter, wearing only light jackets, without gloves or hats, while carrying a heavy piece of lumber.

They would also have to bluff their way past trigger-happy Nazi soldiers at checkpoints along the way, knowing that if their trick failed they would be shot on the spot.

One step at a time, Markus kept telling himself. *Just one step at a time*.

"Markus," gasped Stefan, breaking into his thoughts. "Look up ahead. Nazis!"

Markus had grown up in Bochnia, Poland, in a loving Jewish family with two sisters, Natalka and Manya, and a younger brother, Izak. Each morning, the four children would rise early and, pulling two-wheeled handcarts behind them, make a three-mile (five-kilometer) round-trip to buy milk from the local farmers. Along with their mother, Maria, and father, Schloymen, the kids made butter and cheese and delivered their dairy products door-to-door.

By the time he was eight, Markus stopped going to school so he could work in the family business and be an apprentice to his uncle, a tailor. Like many kids in Bochnia, Markus didn't have big dreams. He just assumed his life would be the same as those of his parents, whose lives were the same as those of *their* parents.

But when Markus was fifteen, he began sensing that life as he knew it was about to change.

The family had heard about the horrors of *Kristallnacht*. The Reichs knew it was only a matter of time before Adolf Hitler's troops invaded Poland. And, the next year, their fears came true.

After the Nazis took control of Bochnia in 1939, all Jews had to register at a central office and wear a distinctive armband, white with a blue Star of David.

Then the reign of terror began.

The Nazis arrested groups of Jews for no reason. Sometimes those arrested were told they would be executed and were forced to stand for hours in suspense, only to be let go. Other times, they were shot. The Nazis took a special pleasure in riding on the backs of Jews, who were forced to crawl on all fours. The Nazis burned synagogues or turned them into stables, warehouses, bathhouses, or even public bathrooms.

In the rampage of persecution throughout Poland, people of all ages were victims of *aktzias* and were taken off the streets or dragged from their homes and ordered to do forced labor, like slaves. They were beaten and stripped of their dignity by being made to clean bathrooms with their bare hands or wash the floor with their own underwear. In many places, the military forced Jews to burn Torah scrolls, Hebrew books, and other religious articles, and then made them sing and dance around the flames and shout that they, the Jews, were to blame for the war.

One summer day in 1940, Markus was walking down the street, past the school, the museum, and the library that the Nazis had ordered closed. He turned down a side street where a monument to a national hero had been destroyed, one of hundreds of monuments in Poland that the German soldiers had smashed. He ignored the signs posted in public places that warned: ENTRANCE IS FORBIDDEN TO JEWS AND DOGS.

Then, from out of nowhere, a German army truck pulled up behind him, and in an instant he was surrounded by five SS officers, their machine guns aimed right at him. "Get in the truck!" the leader ordered him. "Now!"

Dread swept over Markus. If he got into that truck, he knew he would become a slave at best, or at worst a prisoner marked for death. He wanted to run but knew if he bolted, he would get a bullet in his back.

Markus pleaded with them. "Please, don't take me. My family needs me."

"Get in there!"

"Can I at least go home and tell them what's happening to me, maybe get some clothes?"

Watching from across the street, several kids threw stones at Markus and yelled, "Dirty Jew! Dirty Jew!"

An SS officer stuck his machine gun in Markus's back, forcing the teen to climb into the canvas-covered rear of the truck. Already crammed inside were twenty other glum-faced young men. As the truck roared off, the officers closed the flap so none of the prisoners could see where they were going.

A few hours later, they arrived outside the Polish town of Tarnow, the site of a Nazi forced-labor camp that was under construction. From morning until night, under the watchful eyes of armed guards, Markus and the others were put to work building barracks, unloading supplies, and clearing brush. They worked every day, rain or shine, in the blazing summer and in the frigid winter.

One armed guard told Markus, "You know what your payment is? You get to live."

Not everyone did. The work was too exhausting for some, especially because they weren't given much to eat. Their diet was hardly enough to keep them alive. At breakfast all they received was coffee; lunch consisted of a watery soup that contained a few potatoes; dinner was just bread and coffee. Markus often saved some of the bread for breakfast.

One scorching-hot day, Markus got so dizzy that he stumbled and fell while carrying a 100-pound (45-kilogram) sack of cement. He was too worn out to get up. The guard threw water in Markus's face and then kept kicking him until he struggled to his feet.

"Why are you kicking me?" Markus moaned.

"Because you're not moving fast enough!" said the guard with a sneer.

Markus and the others were slaves, not prisoners, although it was hard to tell the difference in the way they were treated. As forced laborers, they wore regular clothes, but always with the Star of David armband, and sometimes toiled far outside the camp, often with local paid laborers.

For nearly two years, Markus tolerated the long days of hard labor, the cruel treatment of the guards, and the lack of decent food. But what bothered him the most was not having any contact with his family. The guards wouldn't let the slaves write letters to their loved ones or tell the relatives where their kidnapped sons were or even if they were still alive. Markus thought about his family every day and would carry on imaginary conversations with them. *God, how I miss them.*

One bone-chilling winter day, Markus and Stefan Schreiber, a fellow work slave from Bochnia, had been building a shed at the edge of the camp. Early in the afternoon, they were waiting for a truck to take them back to the barracks when Markus realized there were no guards in sight.

"Stefan," Markus said, "this is our chance to escape!"

"Are you crazy?" Stefan replied. "If we run off now, we'll have no food, no shelter. The soldiers will follow our tracks in the snow and shoot us."

"We're not going to run," said Markus. "We're going to walk out of here."

"What are you talking about?"

"We're going to walk on the road and pretend we're Polish workers." Pointing to a ten-foot-long (three-meter-long) piece of lumber, he said, "Grab the other end and put it on your shoulder." After they picked it up, Markus, in the rear, said, "Now start walking."

"Where are we going?"

"Home."

And so they began their bold escape in the merciless cold. Stefan started to shiver instantly, more out of worry than because of the bitter winter wind. "This is insane," he said. "Bochnia is more than sixty kilometers [thirty-six miles] away. It'll take us days to get there. We're bound to get caught."

"Don't be so afraid. We're almost dead anyway, so why fear it?"

One step at a time, Markus kept telling himself. *One step at a time.*

They trekked for several hours, the subzero cold making Markus almost wish he was back in the barracks by the wood-burning stove, away from the stinging gusts of wind. But he forgot his agony when Stefan suddenly announced that there was a Nazi checkpoint up ahead. German soldiers stood guard at all the bridges because members of the Polish underground were blowing them up.

"What will we do?" asked Stefan.

"We'll keep walking like we know what we're doing and where we're going," Markus replied.

And so they did. The two escapees walked confidently right past the soldiers, who never said a word to them. The same thing happened at the next bridge and the one after that. Incredibly, day after day not one soldier ever bothered to question them. After all, Markus reasoned, to the soldiers, he and Stefan were just two worthless Jewish workers.

For food, the two boys stopped at farmhouses along the way and begged for something to eat. Farmers always had food. Sometimes the boys were turned away, but they were never turned in to the Nazis. At night, they slept on the ground or sometimes in a barn.

During the day, as they battled the icy wind, they kept marching closer and closer to home, the lumber still on their shoulders.

One step at a time. Just one step at a time.

Markus couldn't tell which pain was worse — his sore shoulder or his frozen skin. He kept his hands in his pockets as best he could and balanced the lumber on his skinny shoulder. Stefan was in much worse shape. His fingers had turned black — a sign that frostbite had set in.

Finally, after more than a week of trudging through the snow and cold, Markus and Stefan reached the outskirts of Bochnia. They learned that all the Jews had been moved to a ghetto in the very neighborhood where Markus's family lived. When the two escapees neared the ghetto, they jubilantly threw the lumber away and, although close to exhaustion, ran toward their homes.

It was the middle of the night when Markus reached his family's house. He was so excited that he could hardly breathe. He walked up to the front door and knocked. He heard his mother timidly ask, "Who is it?"

"Mama, it's Markus!"

His mother let out a scream and whipped open the

door. She looked at the grinning, raw, weather-beaten face of her scrawny son and shrieked, "You've come back from the dead!" Then she slumped into his arms and wept tears of joy. Into the hallway behind her rushed Markus's disbelieving father, sisters, and brother, who sobbed as they hugged and kissed him.

To celebrate his homecoming, Markus's mother made potato pancakes. It was a special treat considering they had little to eat in the house, because the Nazis made it difficult for the Jews in the ghetto to get food. The Nazis wouldn't even let the family continue its dairy business, so there was no way to make money. The Reichs survived with the help of Markus's older sister, Natalka. Because she had blond hair and blue eyes, Natalka didn't look Jewish to the Nazis. So she would sneak out of the ghetto without wearing the Star of David — an action punishable by death — and gather food from Christian friends and smuggle it back to the house.

In order to stay with his family in the ghetto, Markus had to register with the *Judenrat*, a Jewish council that was controlled by the Nazis. Amazingly, the *Judenrat* didn't know he had escaped from the forced-labor camp. The Nazis put him to work along with many of the other Jews in town. Stefan wasn't among them. He had lost most of his fingers to frostbite.

Compared with the forced-labor camp near Tarnow, the work in Bochnia wasn't too bad — except for one sickening day. The Nazis drove Markus and a dozen other Jews to the edge of town and ordered them to dig a trench about fifty yards (forty-six meters) long, two yards (one and three-quarter meters) wide, and one yard (nine-tenths of a meter) deep. When they had finished, they were taken a few blocks away and told to wait. Moments later, they heard machine-gun fire and screams. Then Markus and his fellow workers were brought back to the trench — and ordered to bury the fifty-seven Jews who had just been slain.

Markus wanted to throw up. He wanted to weep. He wanted to kill the soldiers for slaughtering these innocent people. *Get control of yourself,* he told himself. *Don't let them see how you feel or you'll be one of those dead bodies.* So, while battling the rage and heartache inside him, Markus and the other members of the work detail toiled feverishly to cover up the murdered victims. The sooner they finished the ghastly task, the sooner they could go home and cry.

Six months after his return, Markus was walking down the street in Bochnia when once again he was grabbed by the Nazis and taken away. He was sent to another forced-labor camp, this time in Klay, just a few miles outside of town. The camp, built deep in the forest and hidden among tall pine trees, was an ammunition factory that had eight huge warehouses. An electrified barbed-wire fence and watchtowers with armed guards surrounded the camp. About 300 boxcars were loaded and unloaded every day with bombs and land mines. It was Markus's job to carry 100-pound (45-kilogram) bombs to a special place in the forest and stack them up. As in his previous camp, Markus wasn't allowed to communicate with his family. But he did learn tragic news: Those in the Bochnia ghetto, more than 3,000 Jews, had been either murdered or shipped off to a death camp. Markus held little hope that he would ever see his family again. He knew in his heart that he was now an orphan. But by then, there were only a few tears left in him, so he could barely cry.

Markus had been in Klay for six months when he and about a hundred others were marched to a new forced-labor camp, Plaszow, about ten miles (sixteen kilometers) away, just outside of the city of Krakow. During the march, two prisoners managed to escape, which cheered up Markus and gave him hope that someday he would escape again, too.

As the group entered the camp, Markus was thrilled to see that his cousin, Max Hilfstein, was there. They waved to each other, and Markus thought, *Max looks pretty healthy. His clothes aren't even torn. Maybe it won't be so bad here.*

The group was put in a room, where a German colonel stood before them. For several minutes, he kept slapping his riding crop against his spit-shined, knee-high boots and glowered at the prisoners. Finally, he spoke. "I understand that two of your people escaped today during your little walk to Plaszow. I can assure you they didn't get far. I can also assure you that you will meet the same fate they did. You see, when someone in a group escapes, then everyone in the group is punished — by execution."

Gasps, cries, and wails filled the room. Markus felt weak in the knees. *So this is how my life is going to end. I should have joined those two. At least my death would have been quick.*

As Markus waited with the others to be executed, a guard came into the room and tugged at Markus's sleeve. "Come with me."

This is it, thought Markus. *I wonder how I'll die. Will they shoot me or hang me? Maybe gas me? I hope I won't suffer.* The guard shoved him into another room, where about thirty other Jews were huddled together.

Minutes later, Markus heard Max calling to him through a barred window. He went to the window and said, "It's so good to see you, Max!"

"Shhh," whispered Max. "I'm not supposed to be here. I'm a barber, and I do a good job taking care of the officers, so I have some privileges. I convinced a guard to pull you out of the group and put you here so you'll be safe. I'll see you later."

Markus felt so relieved. *I'm not going to die after all!*

But his relief didn't last long. An hour later, Max returned. This time his voice was quivering. "The guard tricked me. Everyone in this room is scheduled to be shot within the hour, just like the first group!"

The news jolted Markus, sending his mind reeling in panic. "I've got to find a way out of here." His eyes darted around the room. Guards were at the door; the windows were barred. It looked hopeless. Then he spotted the latrine. Turning to Max, he murmured, "I'm going to hide under the toilets until it's safe."

"Good idea. I'll return later and knock three times on the latrine wall. That will be your signal to come out."

Markus walked into the latrine. The toilets were nothing more than wooden planks with holes cut out over a trench. When no one was looking, he lifted a plank and jumped into the human waste, which reached up to his armpits. Markus gagged from the stench but remained there, totally still, for hours. He relied on his imagination to get him through the disgusting situation. In his mind, he was lying on his back on a haystack on a farm, watching the clouds drift by on a warm spring day. It was hard, but Markus managed to keep focused on that image.

Finally, he heard three knocks and, with some effort, climbed out of the trench. He found Max, who led him to a special barracks, where he took a shower — the first in several months — and was given some food.

Markus managed to slip into another barracks, taking the place of a prisoner who had died from malnutrition earlier in the day. At Plaszow, prisoners slept twelve to a bunk — three levels with four inmates per mattress. Although it was a forced-labor camp rather than a concentration camp, Plaszow was known for its extreme cruelty to prisoners. The guards even made going to the bathroom at night a terrifying experience.

One night, during his first week there, Markus went to the barracks door and asked the guard for permission to use the latrine, which was in a separate building. The guard told him to step outside.

When Markus did, the guard ordered, "Get down on the ground and start doing push-ups." Markus did as he was told. "Wait," said the guard. "Let's make it more challenging." Then he placed a big bag of rocks on the teenager's back. "Okay, now do your push-ups." Markus's thin muscles shook from the strain. Every time he slowed down, the guard would kick him. For thirty agonizing minutes, Markus did push-ups before the guard got bored and said, "Okay, you can use the latrine."

The next day, when Markus told Max what had happened, Max said, "You were lucky. Sometimes people get beaten up before they're allowed to use the latrine. Or the guards will sit on you and make you crawl." Markus never went to the bathroom at night again.

Months later, the Germans ordered all the prisoners out of Plaszow and into death camps. Markus, Max, and Max's wife, Erna, were part of a group that had to walk thirty miles (forty-eight kilometers) to Auschwitz — a camp that would become the site of the greatest mass murder in history.

During the march, prisoners too feeble to take another step were shot where they fell. Erna, weakened by hunger and illness, began to stumble, so Max carried her until he, too, was exhausted. "I can't carry her anymore, Markus. Help me."

Markus himself was frail and having difficulty walking. But he had to help. After all, Max had saved his life. Here was a chance to repay him. So Markus put Erna on his back — she weighed only eighty pounds (thirty-six kilograms) — and plodded on for a whole day until they arrived at Auschwitz.

So this is where I'm going to die, Markus thought.

For the next three months, he saw people being led to

the gas chambers, people being shot as they stood in formation, people being hanged. And every day he wondered if this would be the last day of his life. Clad in a blue-and-white-striped prison uniform, Markus was nothing but skin and bones. He was beyond fear, beyond even caring.

That's why, when about twenty American planes flew overhead one day and attacked factories near the camp, he lay on his back on the ground and watched the bombs drop with the same fascination he'd felt watching fireworks years earlier, before the war. The explosions were close enough for Markus to feel the ground shake with each strike. He wasn't afraid. In fact, he wished they'd bomb Auschwitz, because he figured it would give him a chance to escape — or put him out of his misery.

"Keep bombing them," he called out to the planes. "And when you're done there, come over and bomb here!"

"Shhh," said Max. "If the guards hear you cheering like that, they'll kill you."

In early 1945, when it was clear the Nazis were losing the war, they tried to remove all traces of the crimes they had committed at Auschwitz. German soldiers began transporting prisoners to other death camps, destroying the gas chambers, and burning documents.

Markus was part of a group that was taken by open boxcar to Dachau, in southern Germany, which was another terrible camp, but they weren't let in because it was too full. So the train chugged on in the dreary, cold winter weather to Czechoslovakia. The prisoners, packed so tightly they couldn't even sit, were licking snow off one another because they had no food or water. As the train went under overpasses, kindhearted Czechoslovakians would throw bread into the open boxcars. Whenever Markus caught bread, he would break it up and share it with others around him. One time, he waved at a woman who had tossed several loaves into the boxcar. As she waved back, smiling, she was shot by a guard.

The train kept going from one town to another, but all the camps were full. Finally, it stopped outside the town of Garching, Germany, where the prisoners were ordered to march in the snow. By now, most of them were too feeble and sick to walk. They began falling to the ground. Sometimes the guards shot them; other times, the guards would just leave them there to die.

They're going to take us into the woods and kill us, thought Markus. *If I try to run, they'll shoot me. My only chance is to play dead.* So Markus flopped into the snow facedown and lay there motionless. He could hear the guards firing rounds into bodies sprawled by the wayside. *Please don't come here, please don't come here.* Suddenly, he heard the crunch of footsteps in the snow heading his way. *Don't move, don't breathe.* His heart was beating so wildly that he was sure the guard would see his body vibrating. Markus held his breath until he thought he would pass out. And then, to his great relief, he heard the footsteps grow fainter. Nevertheless, he remained still for another thirty minutes, because he had heard stories of guards hiding in the bushes, waiting to shoot those prisoners who pretended to be dead but then got up after they thought everyone had left.

Warily, he opened one eye and slowly turned his head. He saw no one. Then he rolled over and made a mad dash for the woods. But the lack of food had taken a terrible toll, and he was too weak to run far.

A short while later, Markus staggered to the outskirts of Garching, starving and shivering. He came upon a building that had eight apartments on the first floor. When he escaped the first time from the camp in Tarnow, he'd always had pretty good luck going up to a strange house and asking for food. *I might as well try it again,* he thought. *But which door?* For no reason in particular, he chose the third door from the left. He knocked and thought, *Wouldn't it be something if a Nazi soldier answers? I made it all the way through the war only to get shot in the final days. . . .*

An angel appeared at the door. She was petite and blond, with soft blue eyes and flawless skin. Markus had never seen such a beautiful young woman before.

But what the woman saw made her flinch. Standing before her was a scraggly, bald young man who weighed less than ninety pounds (forty kilograms), wearing a dirty, torn prison uniform.

"Please," Markus said in German, "Can I have something to eat? I'm very hungry."

The beautiful young woman looked deep into his eyes — eyes, she could tell, that had witnessed years of horror. She knew he was an escaped prisoner, and she knew that, although the war would be over any day now, she still risked death if she helped him. But she couldn't stand the thought of leaving him out in the cold. "Of course, come in," she said at last. She led Markus into the kitchen, where he slumped over the table. "I don't have much — some milk and bread," she said.

"That would be wonderful. Thank you."

Markus wanted to wolf it all down in one gulp, but instead he ate and drank a little at a time, so he could savor every bite. As he ate, the woman introduced herself. Her name was Maria Engelbrecht. She was a German Catholic and a young widow who had lost her husband a year earlier, shortly after the birth of their son, Karl. When Markus finished eating, Maria let him wash up and gave him some fresh clothes that had belonged to her late husband. Then she took him down into the basement and set up a cot so he could sleep. Over the next two days, Maria hid him from her nosy neighbors and tended to him.

And then came the word: "The war is over, Markus," Maria said. "The Americans have arrived here. It's safe now."

Markus went to the new camp the American soldiers had set up. There, he was given food, shelter, and medical care. He learned that all the prisoners who had been taken off the train with him and forced to march were later machine-gunned to death, just as he'd thought they'd be.

Markus stayed at the camp and worked in the kitchen while he regained his strength and health. Every day, he gathered extra food and leftovers from the mess hall and brought them to Maria, because she had been so kind to him. And every day, he got to know her a little bit better, and she got to know him.

A year later, when he had fully recovered and the Americans had closed down their camp, Markus chose to stay with Maria. He wasn't about to leave the woman he would one day marry.

After the war, Markus remained in Garching, working as a tailor. He learned that his entire family had died in death camps.

He came to the United States in 1951 and settled in Asheville, North Carolina, where he became a metal worker and learned English by watching old Western movies. In 1953, he sent for Maria. They married a short time later, and Markus eventually became a successful business owner. They raised Maria's son, Karl, and their daughter, Manya, and now have four grandchildren and live in retirement in Asheville.

Markus's cousin, Max, and Max's wife, Erna, survived the war and moved to New York, where Max became a hairdresser and Erna became a science professor and author.

How Can the Stars Seem So Happy in This Horrible Place?
George and Ursula Levy's Story

George Levy and his little sister, Ursula, squirmed in the living room, shaking their heads, tears streaming down their faces. They were listening to their mother, Lucie, explain why she was sending them off to another country — alone.

"It's no longer safe here," Lucie said to her trembling eight-and-a-half-year-old son and her sobbing daughter, who was a month away from turning four. "I've made arrangements for you to take the transport [train] to Holland, where a nice gentleman will meet you. He has helped hundreds of Jewish children like you escape from Germany."

"But, *Mutti*, we don't want to leave," George protested. "We want to stay here in Lippstadt with you."

"Please, *Mutti*," blurted Ursula.

The children could tell their mother's heart was breaking more with each passing second and that she fought hard to remain strong for them — the two most important people in her life. "It's too dangerous for you to stay," their mother said at last. "The Nazis are making life miserable for Jews here in Germany. You saw what they did to your father."

"Are we bad people?" George asked. "Is that why they killed Father and Uncle Ludwig? Is that why we have to leave?"

Lucie knelt in front of her children, put her arms around them, and said, "Not for one second should you ever think you are bad. You are good. The Nazis are bad. They hate Jews. That's why it's so important that you leave Lippstadt right away."

"Why can't you come?" asked Ursula.

"They passed a law making it difficult for grown-ups like me to leave right now. But I will join you soon. I promise. And then we'll start a new life together. It will be so nice in Holland. You'll make new friends, and we'll get a nice house."

"Will it have a cherry tree?" asked Ursula, wiping her runny nose with the back of her hand. "I like cherry trees."

"Of course," Lucie replied. "It will be such a beautiful tree that in the springtime it will snow pink cherry blossoms."

George's chest heaved from crying. He knew there was nothing more he could do to change his mother's mind. "When do we have to go?" he asked.

Their mother's answer caused both George and Ursula to burst into tears again. "There is a children's transport leaving tomorrow," she said. "We'd better start packing now."

The next morning, a brisk April day in 1939, Ursula and George — each gripping a suitcase stuffed with clothes (Lucie had sewn their initials into each garment) — stood on the platform of the train station. Their sad eyes were locked on their mother, who bent over and dabbed at their tears. The family paid little attention to the hundreds of other frightened children who were also being sent away for their own safety as part of an international effort called *Kindertransport*. It eventually would ship 10,000 German Jewish children, from infants to young teens, to Holland and then onto ferries across the English Channel to Britain, where most had no family or friends but were able to find willing foster families. The Levy children, however, were going only as far as Holland, four hours away.

In the midst of grieving families bidding *auf wiedersehen* (good-bye) to their children, George and Ursula clutched their mother, not wanting ever to let go. The train whistle blew, signaling an immediate departure. Smiling bravely, Lucie told them, "You'll be in good hands . . . and you'll be safe."

Kissing Ursula, Lucie told her, "I'll be there before you know it, and then we'll celebrate your birthday." Turning to George, she said, "You take good care of your sister." George nodded, too choked up to talk. Lucie hugged her children one last time. "I love you so much."

George and Ursula quietly boarded, found seats, and pressed their faces against the window as the train slowly moved out of the station. "Bye, *Mutti*, bye!" they shouted.

Lucie ran alongside the train, waving and smiling, calling out to them. "Everything is going to be all right. We'll be together soon and find a cute house — one with a cherry tree. . . ." She no longer could keep pace with the train and stopped at the end of the platform, where she was surrounded by dozens of weeping parents.

George and Ursula slumped in their seats, listening to sniffling kids around them, too heartbroken to talk.

Finally, Ursula spoke. "George, I'm scared."

George was, too. He just wouldn't admit it. "Let's not talk for a while. Let's look out the window." His mind was still reeling over how quickly life had changed — as quickly as the views that sped past their window.

The Levy children had enjoyed a blissful early childhood with loving parents and an extended family in a three-story apartment house that their father, Max, owned. Max ran a dry-goods store on the main floor of the building, which was located in the center of Lippstadt. But in the summer of 1938, the Nazis began forcing Jews to sell their businesses and homes to German non-Jews for much less than they were worth. The Levys had to move into a home with another family.

Then, in November 1938, came the horrors of *Kristall-*

nacht. Max and his brother, Ludwig, were taken away to a concentration camp and tortured for six weeks. When they were released, they were terribly injured. Ludwig died on Christmas Day. Max managed to hang on a little longer. He died three weeks later.

Through this terrifying misery, Lucie remained strong for her children, blanketing them with warmth, love, and a positive attitude. "Don't worry," she'd say. "Things will get better." She never let on how frightened she was or how much it hurt her to put her beloved children on the train.

After they reached Holland, George and Ursula stayed for a few days at a refugee camp in Rotterdam. Then the man who had arranged their escape, Joseph van Mackelenbergh, took them to the St. Jacobus Children's Home in Eersel. The home, which was run by Catholic nuns, took in malnourished kids from Dutch cities where food was scarce. Every six weeks, a group of 200 children would come to enjoy the country air and good food. They would hike in the forest and on the farm and regain their strength. Then they would be sent home and replaced by another 200. But there were about twenty children who lived full-time in the home — Jews who had fled Germany and were hiding from the Nazis, pretending to be visiting Dutch children.

At first, some of the Dutch kids called the Levys *rot moffen* (rotten Germans). The Levys responded by calling them "cheeseheads." George scuffled with a few who had taunted him, but he soon made friends with them, especially after the nuns made it clear to the children they would not tolerate any mistreatment of the Jews. The Dutch children accepted Ursula, too. Proof came when a boy who had a piece of gum — a rare treat — let Ursula chew on it for a few minutes before passing it on to others.

Although she was treated well at the home, Ursula cried herself to sleep every night during those first few weeks.

One afternoon, Ursula tracked down her brother. "George, follow me," she said. "I want to show you something." She took him by the hand and led him into a nearby field. "Look," she said, pointing to a cherry tree bursting with pink blossoms. "It's just like the one *Mutti* said we'd have when we're all together again. See all the blossoms falling? It looks like pink snow."

The pretty cherry tree was a comfort to Ursula, but she remained homesick and missed her mother deeply. What helped ease her anguish were the postcards Lucie sent the children. Ursula kept the cards — which often had fairy tale characters on the front — under her pillow. Even though she was too young to read, she memorized the words after George read aloud their mother's messages. All the cards carried the same basic thought: "I hope that you're having a good time and getting enough to eat. I'm doing fine and will be joining you soon." She ended each card, "Be nice to each other. George, make sure you take care of your sister."

For the next year, Lucie's cards kept coming, always

with the promise that she would be arriving soon in Holland. Lucie just couldn't bring herself to tell her children the truth — that the laws in Germany had been tightened, making it almost impossible for her to leave.

Life for the children at the home followed a strict regimen of healthy meals, vigorous hikes, school, and plenty of sleep. While Ursula went to kindergarten, George attended classes in Eersel and learned Dutch until he could speak without an accent.

The two received extra attention from Father Leo Weyers, the rector who supervised the home. The kindly priest became something of a father figure to the two lonely children. On Sundays, dressed in their best clothes, George and Ursula had dinner at his house.

On May 10, 1940, one day before Ursula's fifth birthday, Germany invaded Holland. It took only four days for the Nazis to take over the country. To Ursula, who still didn't fully understand what danger they were in, it was exciting to see German planes roaring overhead and waves of Nazi soldiers marching in unison, while others rode grandly on horseback. To George, who knew how deadly their situation was, it was terrifying.

In 1941, the Nazis in Holland ordered all Jews, including children, to wear a large yellow Star of David on their right arm with the word *Jood* (Dutch for "Jew") in its center. At first, wearing the star to school embarrassed George and Ursula. But none of their fellow students seemed to care, so, after a while, neither did the Levys.

However, George and Ursula were becoming increasingly troubled because they hadn't received a postcard from their mother in months. They knew she never would have stopped writing to them unless something terrible had happened.

Soon, they learned that it had.

"I don't know any easy way to tell you this," one of the nuns said to George in the fall of 1942. "We have reason to believe your mother is dead."

There were no details given of where or when or how she might have died. Not that it mattered to George, because knowing the details wouldn't bring her back, wouldn't lessen the pain in his heart, wouldn't change the fact that he and his sister were now orphans.

Maybe that's not such a bad thing, George told himself. Maybe now, he figured, he wouldn't feel so disappointed when another week went by without a card from *Mutti* or another month went by without her showing up in Holland as she had promised. He could stop worrying about her. He had just turned twelve, and as the big brother, he could now worry only about his welfare and that of his seven-year-old sister. The first decision George made as the head of this two-person family was not to tell Ursula.

In March 1943, the Levys were called into Father Weyers's office. His usual smile had been replaced by a grim, nervous look. In the room was the chief of police of Eersel.

"My dear children," the priest said. "I have received an order from officials that you two are to be deported to Camp Vught."

"What does that mean?" asked George, thinking that whatever it was, it didn't sound good.

The police chief said, "It is a camp for Jews about twenty kilometers [twelve miles] from here. I'm sorry, but I have no choice but to carry out the order of the government."

"When do we leave?" George asked.

"In the morning," the police chief answered promptly. "I will send two policemen to pick you up." Then, turning to the priest, he said, "The men will be in plainclothes so the children won't look like criminals."

That was little comfort to George, who began to cry. At the first sign of his tears, Ursula began bawling, too. St. Jacobus had been their home and their security for nearly four years, and they didn't want to leave. George wanted to shout to Father Weyers, "In the name of God, help us!" But George could tell by the pitiful look on the priest's face that he was powerless.

The next morning, distressed nuns gathered around the two children and hugged them. Ursula's favorite nun, Sister Brigitte, whispered to her, "I wish I could go in your place."

Father Weyers gave them a special blessing and handed each a holy card that had a poem on one side:

By night and by day,
In all kinds of wind and weather,
God's angel will be by your side.
Even if you stray far away from home,
He will bring you safely home again.

The faith expressed in that holy card — that they would one day return home — was severely tested the moment George and Ursula arrived at Vught, the Nazis' first major concentration camp in Holland. The children didn't know that this was a holding station where the fate of each prisoner was decided within a month or two. Those too young or too old to work were sent to Auschwitz in Poland to die immediately in the gas chambers, while the "luckier ones" were shipped to Bergen-Belsen in Germany to die slowly from starvation or disease.

Once inside the high barbed-wire fences and moat that surrounded the camp, George was sent to the men's barracks and Ursula to the women's. Ursula felt totally alone and abandoned, and she cried day and night. Only on Sundays was George able to visit with her for a few hours.

It was in Camp Vught that the Levys first witnessed the shocking brutality of Nazi guards, especially Officer Etlinger. He would ride his bicycle through the camp and randomly hit inmates over the head with a club just for the fun of it. When a prisoner protested after seeing a friend clubbed, Etlinger gave him twenty-five lashes with a whip — while forcing the rest of the inmates to watch.

Etlinger used any excuse to hurt people. Once, during an inspection in the women's barracks, he examined every bed to see if it was made neatly, with the blanket taut and tucked. Whip in hand, he clomped down the middle of the barracks, past Ursula, carefully eyeing each bed. He stopped at one woman's bed and picked up a tiny piece of lint. "What is this?" he thundered, his reddened face so close to the woman's that his nose touched hers. "A piece of lint? Get down on the floor!"

She dropped down on her stomach. "I want everyone to look and see what happens when I find filth in this barracks," he barked. Then he cracked his whip across the woman's back. Ursula cringed and wanted to turn her head, but she was afraid that if she did, he would notice and then she would feel the sting of his whip.

After weeks of seeing constant brutality and standing for hours every day at *appell* (roll call) in all kinds of weather, Ursula wondered if she would ever laugh or smile again.

On Ursula's eighth birthday, she and George were called into the commandant's office. When they walked in and saw a familiar face, they shouted in glee. There, standing next to the commandant, was Joseph van Mackelenbergh, the man who had arranged for their escape from Germany to Holland. They rushed up and hugged him but suddenly backed off when they saw Officer Etlinger seated in the corner of the room.

"Happy birthday, Ursula," Joseph said.

"You remembered my birthday?" Ursula asked.

"But of course. You and George are my favorite young people. My hardware store isn't too far from the camp, so when I realized it was your birthday, I came right over to celebrate it with you and George. I brought you some treats to share." Looking at George, Joseph asked, "And how are you?"

"I'm fine, sir."

Officer Etlinger then motioned for Ursula to come over to him. When she did — but only after an uncomfortable hesitation — he set her on his knee. "You're doing fine here, aren't you?" the officer asked her.

Terrified, Ursula nodded. Having this cruel man touch her made her shudder. Chills slithered up her spine as the hands that had clubbed and whipped prisoners caressed her hair. She wanted to scream and run into Joseph's arms and beg him to take her away. But she didn't. She smiled instead.

"I told the commandant about your American father," Joseph said to George and Ursula. "He's now working at a hospital in Chicago. He says being a doctor there has kept him very busy, but not so busy that he doesn't miss you every minute of every day. He goes to Mass and prays for your safety." He stared at Ursula and then at George as he spoke slowly and deliberately.

American father? Doctor? Chicago? What's he talking about? Ursula wondered. *We've got an uncle in Chicago who's a doctor.* But judging by the way Joseph looked at her and George, she knew better than to say anything. *Maybe George knows what's going on.*

George sensed that Joseph was secretly signaling him to go along with the lie. Joseph then handed the commandant a document that "proved" that the Levys' father was American. The German didn't know that the paper had been forged.

"I guess you could have some Aryan blood in you,"

Etlinger said to Ursula. Then, glancing at George, he added, "You, too, because you have blue eyes."

Joseph's visit was much too short to suit the Levys. They had felt safe while he was there. As Joseph prepared to leave, he promised to visit them again. Then the commandant said to him, "I will be shopping at your store again soon. I expect to be given the same large discount as before, right?"

"But of course."

As they headed back to the barracks, George criticized Ursula. "How could you sit on the lap of that monster Etlinger?" he demanded in disgust.

"What was I supposed to do?" Ursula countered. "Say no? He would have hit me. Maybe not in the office, but later. I was shaking the whole time. I hated every second." Her eyes filled with tears.

George nodded. "Don't cry. I'm sorry."

"Why was Mr. van Mackelenbergh lying about our father?" Ursula asked through her tears. "He knows Father is dead."

"Because he's trying to save us," explained George. "That paper he had was false. He was telling us, without saying it, to lie. From now on, we will tell everyone we have a German Jewish mother and an American Catholic father. Half Jews with an American parent get treated better. That's why he made up that story. I think the reason he was able to see us — regular people aren't allowed to visit the camp — is because he bribed the commandant by selling him things in his store for next to nothing."

Joseph's bribery worked. Instead of being deported to another camp, as most of the prisoners were within two months, the Levys were transferred to a nicer barracks that housed a privileged group — the diamond cutters — whose services the Nazis needed.

The commandant also assigned a woman prisoner named Florence to act as the Levys' guardian. She kept an eye on them and made sure they didn't get into any trouble. Not that Ursula ever would. She had learned instinctively to remain invisible and be quiet and obedient. She didn't ever want to be noticed by the guards.

Ursula was more comfortable in the diamond cutters' barracks because she was once again with her big brother. They were able to roam around the camp and even had the use of a beat-up old piano. George, who had taken piano lessons, tried to teach his sister how to play. He also gave her math lessons by using a stick to draw numbers and problems in the dirt.

But Ursula sensed that she was becoming a drag on her brother, always hanging around him, never wanting to be alone. The strain of being imprisoned in this awful place magnified their growing annoyance with each other. Their tensions finally came to a head one day when Ursula whined to him, "Quit bossing me around. Just because you're bigger than me doesn't mean you can always tell me what to do."

George exploded. "If it wasn't for you holding me back, I would have been out of here long ago! I would have escaped!" he shouted. They both knew it wasn't true. No one ever escaped Camp Vught. Ursula dashed off, found a corner where no one would see her, and cried.

Later, hoping to win back George's favor, Ursula decided to make him a little dumpling for his upcoming birthday. She began saving scraps of food under her pillow — a slice of potato, a piece of bread. But soon she realized that the tidbits she had saved wouldn't make much of a dumpling — besides, how was she going to cook a dumpling? — so she ate them. Meanwhile, she made an effort to give her big brother more space to be alone.

For a reason that George himself couldn't explain, he sometimes visited the transit area, where raw emotions churned in a tempest of tears, wails, and shouts. It was a horrid place where families were torn apart. They were given ten minutes to say good-bye before family members were separated, put on trucks to the train station, and sent by rail to different camps. Loved ones wept and screeched and clutched at one another while guards beat them and yanked them away. The final destination for many: the gas chambers of Auschwitz.

It was painful to watch, but George felt a need to witness these scenes of unimaginable sorrow and anguish. He watched so he would never forget.

I'm glad Mutti is dead so I don't have to say good-bye like this and see her being taken away, George would think. *At least if it happens to me, Ursula and I would go together. There won't be any good-byes.*

George didn't know it, but his sister watched, too, from afar. She had her own reason for being there — to witness the strength of the human spirit. Ursula never ceased to be awed by the unbendable will and strong faith of the prisoners, who broke out in song as they waited for the last person to board the crammed transport trucks. The strains of the uplifting Dutch song "Oh, I Wish It Were True, Then I Would Have Joy in My Life" echoed throughout the camp. As the prisoners headed off to their doom, they raised their voices in farewell by singing the Hebrew song "Eliahu Hanavi," praising the prophet Elijah. Hearing this, Ursula found strength and inspiration. The Jews had scored a moral triumph over their Nazi tormentors.

One day, while George was at the transit area, he heard officials call the guardian Florence's name on the transport list. Panic-stricken, Florence pleaded with Etlinger that this was a terrible mistake. "I can't go," she begged. "I'm in charge of the Levy children."

Etlinger dragged Florence over to George and asked him, "Do you need her?"

The flustered boy felt paralyzed and didn't know what to do. *If I say no, they're going to take her away. If I say yes, they might make Ursula and me go with her.*

"Tell him, George," Florence cried, her eyes pleading for his help. "Tell him how I look after you two and make sure you get fed and stay healthy and safe. Please!"

"Well, answer me!" Etlinger shouted.

Think! Think! Say something before he beats you! Suddenly the words tumbled out in a rush, unleashed by George's survival instinct. "No, we don't need her. I'm old enough to take care of my sister and myself."

"George, no! No! How could you? You need me!" Florence shrieked, flailing as Etlinger hauled her away.

George, sick to his stomach, ran off and sobbed. For days he was unable to get Florence's high-pitched screams out of his mind.

Then, in October 1943, the Levys' names were called. But instead of being sent straight to Auschwitz, they were transported to Westerbork, a camp in northern Holland. There they stayed in an orphanage run by religious Jewish prisoners, who conducted a school where math and Hebrew were taught. Ursula especially enjoyed Friday evenings, when they celebrated the Sabbath and sang Jewish songs. She admired the camp's religious leaders because, despite their suffering, they remained steadfast in their devotion to God. This faith helped strengthen Ursula's belief that she and George would survive.

After four months at Westerbork, in the winter of 1944, the Levy children were herded onto a train with hundreds of other Jews and shipped back to Germany, thirty-six miles (fifty-eight kilometers) northeast of Hanover, to the notorious Bergen-Belsen concentration camp.

Ursula and George were considered lucky because they were put in a section known as the *Sternlager*, or Star Camp. It housed those prisoners who had connections with the United States or its allies and might one day be exchanged for imprisoned German citizens. *Sternlager* inmates could dress in their own clothes — but had to keep a yellow Star of David on their chest — instead of the striped uniforms of the prisoners in the rest of Bergen-Belsen. But everyone had only one set of clothes and there were no laundry facilities, so their clothes were dirty, smelly, and tattered. George wore the same shirt, jacket, pair of pants, and underwear, and Ursula wore the same checkered black-and-white woolen dress, long stockings, shoes, and coat every day.

The two lived in the men's barracks, which held sixty people; Ursula was the only girl. The Levys shared the same bed — the middle of a triple-decker bunk. Each bed had wooden slats that held a thin straw mattress and blanket. Because there was no heat, prisoners would steal slats from the bunks and burn them to stay warm, but that meant the mattresses sagged from lack of support underneath.

When they first arrived, Ursula and George gasped as wagons piled with dead bodies were paraded past. The horrible scene was repeated daily, reminding all the starving prisoners that one day soon they, too, might join that ghastly parade.

Once a week, the guards would give each prisoner a cigarette. George would trade his and Ursula's to a prisoner named Izzy for Izzy's piece of bread.

"Why are you willing to swap your bread for some smokes, Izzy?" George asked. "You're going to die if you don't eat."

"I'm going to die anyway," replied Izzy. "It's pretty sad, isn't it, that now my greatest joy in life is taking a few puffs from a cigarette? I have nothing else to look forward to."

Izzy died a few weeks later.

For the prisoners, there was little to do, although everyone had to take part in *appell*. The days were filled with unbearable hours of standing endlessly for roll call in mud and rain, snow and ice. SS guards stationed in watchtowers around the camp kept their guns pointed at the inmates night and day. Even though escape was impossible, all the prisoners had to line up for roll call every morning, standing in rows of five to show that none had escaped. The guards had to make the count come out perfectly, minus those who had died during the night. If a single person was unaccounted for, the guards would start the roll call all over again, making the prisoners stand sometimes for a whole day without food or water or a chance to relieve themselves. The guards often found some excuse to claim that the numbers were not correct just so they could start over again.

Most inmates stood with their heads down and their arms wrapped around their chests to stay warm. Shifting from one foot to the other, they shivered in freezing temperatures as their tormentors, clad in warm coats, shouted insults and commands. Sick and starving prisoners would fall over dead, sometimes in front of George and Ursula.

Like all the other inmates, the Levys were always hungry, always cold. Every day the prisoners received a cup of chicory coffee for breakfast, a bowl of watery rutabaga soup for lunch, and bread in the evening. It was just enough to keep them alive so they would die slowly. Although it would have been easy for any man in the barracks to steal the children's bread, no one ever did.

George was constantly looking for food. He carried his spoon with him everywhere in case he had a chance for a few sips of soup when someone wasn't looking. He was so hungry, he sometimes ate wood. If there had been a blade of grass or a weed anywhere on the barren ground, he would have eaten it.

Hunger played havoc with George's mind, one time making him reckless. Once, he noticed a pile of potatoes near the mess hall. *They look so good,* he thought. *Ursula says she's always dreaming about eating potatoes. They would taste delicious and fill our stomachs.* George knew that if he got caught stealing a potato, he'd likely be shot on the spot. *It's worth the risk.* He scanned the area. *Good. The guards aren't looking.* He grabbed a couple of potatoes and swiftly stuffed them under his coat.

"You! Stop right there!" bellowed a guard, leveling his rifle at George. "I saw what you did."

That's it. I'm dead, thought George. He threw the potatoes back into the pile. "I'm sorry, sir. I'm just so hungry."

The guard kept his rifle aimed at the terrified youth. Then he lowered his weapon and growled, "Don't ever let me catch you doing that again, or you'll have a stomach full of bullets."

In the prison next to the *Sternlager* was a fenced-in compound of men who had been transported from Auschwitz. At night, George would sneak over to the fence and ask the inmates there for any news they had learned in Auschwitz about relatives of prisoners in his barracks. The information they gave him was almost always bad news. The years of Nazi brutality had numbed George, so when he returned to his barracks, he often delivered the tragic reports to his fellow prisoners with little sensitivity: "Your wife is dead" or "They gassed your daughter."

There was always a risk whenever George went on these fact-finding missions late at night. Once, a guard snagged him. "What are you doing here?" demanded the guard, his rifle aimed right at George.

Thinking quickly, George replied, "Looking for food. I'm so hungry I have to have something to eat. I can't stand it anymore. I have a little sister, and we're all alone here."

The guard lowered his weapon and said, "I don't have anything to give you, but come back tomorrow night."

The following evening, the guard tossed him a piece of bread. George raced back to the barracks and showed Ursula. "Look what I got." He split it and took the bigger piece, as he always did whenever he divided their rations. *It's my job to take care of her,* he told himself. *I need the energy and, besides, I'm bigger than she is.* But no matter how he rationalized it, George always felt bad that he ate more, even though it wasn't very much more, than his little sister.

George and Ursula had an unpleasant nightly ritual of picking lice off the seams in their clothes and squeezing them with their fingers. Everyone in the camp had lice. As they sat in their bed doing this one night, George told

Ursula, "We have to stay positive, because it's the only way we can survive. I'm hearing from the other prisoners that the Nazis are losing the war. It's only a matter of time. We just need to hold on. Can you do that, Ursula?"

She nodded. "I can do that. I know we're going to make it."

George took out an old comb that he had found one day in the dirt and combed Ursula's wispy hair, which, from lack of nutrition, was now nearly as gray as his. "I like when you do that, George," his sister told him. "Do you think I'll ever have brown hair again?"

"Sure you will. And I will, too. Things will never get back to the way we were, but one day soon we'll be able to move on with our lives."

"When I get out of here, I'm going to eat and eat until I burst," said Ursula. "I'm going to have all the potatoes I want. And then I'm going to move into a cute little house with a big cherry tree in the garden."

When George had finished combing her hair, they took turns rubbing each other's back, as they did every night. Then they lay down, their heads on opposite ends of the saggy, dirty mattress. As she drifted off to sleep, Ursula tried to keep fresh in her mind images of her mother: the sense of security she felt nestled in bed next to *Mutti*, the smell of *Mutti*'s favorite perfume, the sound of her voice singing children's songs, the fuzziness of her favorite coat with the fur collar that Ursula called "kitty cat." It seemed so long ago. As the months dragged on in

Bergen-Belsen, and Ursula's body and mind weakened, the memories of another time and another place faded away.

On summer nights, Ursula would lie on the ground and gaze up at the stars and the moon. *They look so peaceful and beautiful, shining like that. How can the stars seem so happy in this horrible place? I wish George and I could fly out of here, and join them, and sparkle in the sky.*

By the beginning of 1945, the Germans were retreating, and conditions at Bergen-Belsen were worsening. Built to handle a few thousand, the camp was receiving prisoners from other concentration camps and now had a population of more than 40,000. The meager food supply had to be stretched even further, which meant that the only food prisoners received was a small piece of bread once every two days. Adding to their misery, epidemics of the life-threatening diseases typhoid and typhus raged throughout the camp, killing hundreds a day.

Time was running out for the Levys. George was fourteen years old, yet he weighed only seventy-six pounds (thirty-four kilograms). Nine-and-a-half-year-old Ursula was nothing more than a walking skeleton. "We have to hang on just a little bit longer," George would constantly tell his sister. "I'm hearing reports that the Allies are driving back the Nazis. Those planes flying overhead every day lately, those are American and British bombers. It won't be long now."

Later that spring, on April 10, the Nazis began moving prisoners out of Bergen-Belsen. George and Ursula were ordered onto a train bound for Theresienstadt, in Czechoslovakia. None of the inmates knew that the Nazis at Theresienstadt were preparing to gas them.

While 2,500 prisoners — many of them dying from illness and starvation — were loaded into boxcars, George grabbed Ursula's hand and snaked his way through the crowd and onto one of the train's few passenger cars. It was too crowded to sit, but at least they were inside and out of the cold.

Their journey became a drawn-out, aimless trip that, for dozens of prisoners a day, ended in death. For thirteen days, the train rumbled south and north, trapped between the German defenses and the advancing ranks of the Allied forces. The Dutch called it *de dodentrein* — the train of the dead.

The train chugged slowly through the forest and countryside, stopping several times a day because of Allied bombing up ahead or mechanical breakdowns. The prisoners had nothing to eat or drink, so when they were allowed off to relieve themselves, they searched along the tracks for grass or plants to eat and slurped water from puddles. But at every stop, more bodies were taken off the train and buried by the side of the tracks. In fact, so many people died in the passenger cars that the Levys were able to find seats.

At one stop, Ursula stayed on board while George went in search of food, hoping to find a fruit tree he could shake to collect its bounty. The task wasn't easy, because he was so weak and it was hard for him to walk. To his delight,

George found a shriveled apple on the ground. Just then, he heard the train start to move. He looked around. *No guards. Here's my chance to escape! I could hide out in the woods and wait for the Allies to show up. They'll be here in no time, and then I'll be free.* The train started to gain a little momentum. *But what about Ursula? I can't run off and leave her all alone. She's my little sister. She depends on me.* George started to run, but he was so feeble that his knees buckled, and he crashed to the ground. He scrambled to his feet and lurched forward, running as fast as he could until he grabbed a handrail and swung himself onto the steps of the last passenger car.

"Where have you been? I was so worried!" Ursula cried.

"I brought you a present." George showed her the apple and broke it in two. This time, he gave her the bigger piece.

American fighter planes attacked the train more than once, because it was also carrying a German army detachment. The train would screech to a stop, allowing the passengers and soldiers to scramble off and hide under the cars or lie prone against the railroad embankment. Although the raids were frightening for George and Ursula, they understood that these were signs that the end of the war was near.

On April 23, the train stopped again, this time for good. From the front of the train to the back, passengers spread the wonderful news: "We're free! We're free!" The Soviet army had seized the train and captured the Nazi guards.

George had dreamed of this moment for years. He always imagined that upon learning the war was over, he would hop around like a frenzied rabbit and whoop for joy. He would be so happy that he would twirl his little sister in the air and give her a big kiss. But the reality was far different. Like all the surviving passengers, he and Ursula were too frail and exhausted to do much more than smile and shed a few tears of relief, although inside they were elated.

Their liberation came just in time to rekindle the last spark of life left in the prisoners, but it was too late for the hundreds who had died on the train.

"The town of Trobitz is only a kilometer away," a Soviet officer told the freed prisoners. "Go there and occupy any house you want and help yourself to any food you can find."

The survivors staggered into the village, which was deserted because the people there feared the Soviets and had fled. Some villagers had defiantly burned their homes rather than let them fall into the hands of the enemy.

George and Ursula joined a family of prisoners and took over a three-room house similar to the one Ursula had dreamed of living in with her mother and brother. It even had a cherry tree in the backyard, although it hadn't yet bloomed. Giddy with their first breath of freedom, the children found a cart and went from house to house, helping themselves to potatoes, canned milk, cheese, and other assorted goodies, leaving plenty behind for other survivors. They brought their treasure trove of food back to the house to share.

Although George and Ursula were tempted, they knew better than to gorge themselves, because after years of starvation, eating too much food at once could make them seriously ill.

The Soviets soon brought order to the town, but there was little they could do to stop the mounting death rate. The freed prisoners were still dying by the hundreds from typhus, a severe infectious disease transmitted by lice. Of the 2,500 prisoners who had boarded the train in Bergen-Belsen, only 600 were still alive.

The Soviets did their best to delouse the survivors by fumigating their clothes with DDT and shaving off their hair. In the barber's chair, Ursula howled so loudly in protest that the barber cut her hair short but didn't shave it off as he did for the others.

The precautions didn't help the Levys — they both contracted typhus. George got it first. The illness began with a dark red rash, followed by a high fever, stupor, and restlessness. For four days, he thrashed in bed with a fever of 104 degrees. A Soviet doctor arrived and told George, "I have no medicine to cure you. You either make it or you don't." He handed George a chocolate bar, saying, "Take this. It has caffeine, which can help keep your heart beating." The worst soon passed, and George slowly began to recover.

Then the vicious disease struck Ursula, leaving her on the brink of death. The boiling fever ravaged her frail body, pitching her into a semiconscious world of confusion and delusions for days. Whatever grit had helped her survive the previous six years was just enough to pull her through, because on May 11, 1945 — her tenth birthday — she began feeling better. Finally, when she had regained enough strength to get out of bed, she stepped out into the garden for the first time in weeks. What she saw filled her with renewed hope: The cherry tree was ablaze with vibrant pink blossoms shimmering in the sunshine.

"George," Ursula called out, not taking her eyes off the blossoms, "we're going to be just fine."

In June 1945, George and Ursula took a train to Holland, where they were reunited with Joseph van Mackelenbergh. He fed and clothed them and took them to the hospital, where they were treated for malnutrition. They returned to St. Jacobus Children's Home in Eersel and attended school there, once again enjoying Sunday dinners with Father Weyers.

Soon, the children learned a disturbing fact: Their mother had not died in 1942 as George had been told. She had been in German labor camps throughout the war but had died of typhus at the Stutthof concentration camp near Danzig, Poland, just weeks before the camp was liberated in May 1945.

In April 1947 — almost exactly eight years to the day after the Levy children left their hometown of Lippstadt on the Kindertransport — they boarded a plane for Chicago to live with their uncle and aunt, Dr. Joseph and Irmgard Mueller.

Adopting the last name Mueller, George graduated from St. Mary's College in Minnesota, was drafted into the U.S. Army, became an American citizen, got married, and made a living as a salesman and musician. In 1971, he graduated from the University of Illinois College of Pharmacy and became the owner of a pharmacy. George, who lives in Glen Ellyn, Illinois, now works part-time for the Veterans Administration. He and his wife, Katie, raised five children and have fifteen grandchildren.

In 1954, when he was in the army, George went back to Eersel, Holland, to revisit his past. He has returned to Holland several times since. During a 1985 visit, he learned that Florence, the woman who had looked after the Levys in Vught, had survived, so he contacted her. She told him she did not blame him for his role in her deportation.

Following her arrival in America, Ursula also changed her surname to Mueller, at her aunt and uncle's urging. After obtaining her citizenship, she became a nurse, got married, and went on to earn a graduate degree in psychiatric nursing from the University of Illinois while raising two children. She worked in the Chicago public school system from 1968 to 1991 as a teacher nurse. Ursula, who officially changed her last name back to Levy in 1991, lives in Skokie, Illinois, and is now a school volunteer in health education with an emphasis on violence prevention.

Ursula has returned to Holland several times to express her gratitude to the Dutch people who helped save her and George. She has remained close friends with two of her classmates, whom she first met in kindergarten in Eersel. In 1995, for the fiftieth anniversary of the liberation of Holland and Germany, she returned to Europe and spoke to schoolchildren in Germany about her Holocaust experiences.

Both George and Ursula continue to maintain a long-distance friendship with Joseph van Mackelenbergh's family in Holland.

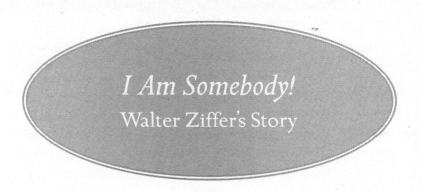

I Am Somebody!
Walter Ziffer's Story

Walter Ziffer woke up on the morning of September 1, 1939, to the booming sounds of thunder. Unfortunately, what he heard wasn't *really* thunder. It was the rumbling of distant artillery shells. Rushing to the window of his family's apartment, the twelve-year-old boy saw nothing but chaos, confusion, and commotion.

In the main street below, he saw shouting Polish soldiers and screaming, frightened citizens rushing past in panic. Horses, straining from pulling wheeled heavy artillery, galloped on the cobblestones alongside speeding army trucks and motorcycles whose tires squealed as they turned the corners. Peasants in rickety wooden carts and on foot quickly herded their goats and cows. It looked like the whole world was retreating from a terror not yet seen.

But the terror was real. The German army had just invaded Poland.

Walter soon heard the dire news that spread throughout the town: Thousands of Nazi troops, backed by high-speed Panzer tanks and planes loaded with bombs, had blasted holes in the Polish lines, destroying communications and preventing the poorly equipped Polish army from moving soldiers, supplies, and ammunition to the front. One by one, the towns in southern Poland quickly fell to the highly mechanized German invasion known as a *blitzkrieg*, or lightning-fast, violent attack.

Now the Nazis were advancing straight toward Walter's hometown of Cesky Tesin, a historic city of about 40,000 people. For about two hours that fateful morning, as Walter watched from his window, the air swirled with the clamor and clatter of ragged Polish soldiers and panicked citizens fleeing north through the city. And then came the silence. A creepy stillness, like the calm before a storm, settled over the deserted streets of Cesky Tesin. It was an unnatural quiet, one that left Walter feeling even more jittery as the minutes ticked away.

An hour later, Walter began to hear a new sound, one that grew louder by the second. It was the growl of engines, lots of them. Before long, German army trucks, tanks, and motorcycles roared down Main Street in perfect rows. Then the silence returned, only to be ruptured half an hour later by a rhythmic *thump, thump, thump*. Peering out his window, Walter saw hundreds of rifle-toting German troops marching in neat columns in flawless harmony, their polished black boots striking the pavement at exactly the same time. *Thump, thump, thump.* To Walter, the parade of ramrod-straight, stern-faced Nazi soldiers was both impressive and scary.

He tried not to worry about himself and his sister, Edith, who was four years older; or his father, Leo, a well-respected attorney; or his mother, Anny. Although the Ziffers were Jews living in an undercurrent of anti-Semitism, Walter's father always tried to ease the family's concerns. Leo would remind them that he had studied law in Vienna and had represented dozens of Germans in lawsuits, and he assured them that the Ziffers had nothing to fear.

But Walter had doubts. He remembered how Franzl, a distant cousin from Vienna, had come to their home and told them how the Nazis had tortured him. Leo had sent the children out of the room, but Walter had secretly peeked around the corner and seen Franzl take off his shirt, revealing wounds on his chest and back where the Nazis had put out their cigarettes on him. Adding to Walter's uneasiness were the times that he and his Jewish friends had been pelted with stones by fellow students, who called them "stinking Jews." And there were those Sunday afternoons when aunts and uncles came to play cards and talked about rumors of Nazi brutality.

Still, Walter's father refused to believe the Germans could act so horribly against fellow citizens just because they were Jewish. That's what Walter wanted to believe, too. After all, Walter figured, his dad was the head of the local Jewish community and was well-liked and well-read, so if anyone knew the truth, it would be Leo. He was a thoughtful, loving, optimistic man who put his family first.

The Ziffers lived comfortably on the top floor of a building that housed a grocery store on the main level and the owners' home on the second floor. The Ziffers' apartment was adorned with expensive furniture, rugs, and shelves filled with books. It was a home in which Walter and Edith felt loved and secure.

But that emotional shield of protection began to crack as soon as the Germans arrived. The day after they took over the city, the Gestapo set up headquarters on the second floor of the Ziffers' building, forcing out the owners. For Walter and Edith, it was quite disturbing to have the Germans living right below them. The worst was the way that the SS officers would laughingly push or trip the kids when they were walking down the stairs.

The Gestapo soon made Leo the head of a council of Jewish leaders, or *Judenrat*. The Nazis would issue orders that the *Judenrat* would pass on to the Jewish citizenry of the town, such as the requirement that all Jews wear a white armband with a blue Star of David on it.

Ten days after the invasion, an SS officer came to the Ziffer apartment and told Leo, "You and your family must get out of here. We can't have you living above us."

Walter, Edith, and Anny sat dumbfounded in the living room. Leo spoke up: "But this is our home."

"It *was* your home. You have twenty-four hours to leave."

The officer turned his back to Leo and ambled through the apartment. The officer began opening closet doors, sifting through clothes, and pulling out dresses and coats. "My daughters will enjoy these very much," he said, ignoring the muffled protests from Edith and her mother. As he started to leave, the officer spotted a camera on a shelf. He picked it up and examined it carefully.

Walter knew how much that camera meant to his father, who was a photography buff. Walter's heart began to sink as the officer continued to admire it. *Don't take that,* Walter thought. *Please don't.*

"You know, Herr Ziffer, my son's birthday is next week," the officer said. "I think this will make a nice birthday gift for him." Then, cradling the camera and the clothes he had taken from the closets, the officer walked out, saying, "You have until noon tomorrow to be gone from here."

Leaving their furniture and most of their possessions behind, the Ziffers hastily gathered up some of their belongings and moved to the apartment house of Leo's brother two blocks away. They managed to hide many of their books, oil paintings, and valuable Persian rugs with a cook who used to work for them before the war. Walter brought along his cherished set of wrenches, which he had bought with money he had earned making spare keys for the neighbors.

For Walter and his family, it was the beginning of a trail of tears — of being forced by the Nazis to move from place to place.

Eventually, under orders from the Nazis, the Ziffers and the town's 1,000 other Jews ended up living in a farm complex on the edge of town. Inside a large dance hall, each family had a twelve-foot by twelve-foot cubicle formed by sheets hanging down from cords strung above the floor. The Ziffers' "home" was up on the stage, where they slept on mattresses on the floor. No one could get in or out of this ghetto without a permit.

The family remained close and loving and tried to maintain a sense of normalcy. Wanting to keep his children's minds sharp, Leo gave Walter and Edith lessons in math, science, history, and English. Walter also spoke Czech and German. Leo reminded them that they were Czechoslovakian, born on the Czech side of the river that had divided Cesky Tesin before Poland took it over in 1938. And he gave them two pieces of advice: "Always do your best . . . and never forget that you are somebody."

Walter, who was fascinated by mechanical things, spent his spare time taking apart the engine of an old abandoned truck to see how it worked. But his tinkering ended when a Gestapo officer came by and stared at Walter's tool set. Walter had seen that look before — in the eyes of the officer who had taken his father's camera.

The Nazi picked up the box of wrenches. "Very nice," he said to Walter as Anny looked on. "I could use these at home."

"But those are mine," Walter protested.

"Not anymore."

Anny begged the Nazi, "Please, my boy needs those tools. He bought them with his own hard-earned money."

"That's a good lesson to learn, about the rewards of hard work," the officer said softly. Then he snarled, "Well, here's another lesson: You Jews own nothing!" He spun on his heel and walked off with the wrenches. Walter was still young enough that he let himself break down in tears.

The Nazis were beginning to deport Jews, but Leo managed to delay deportation for Walter, Edith, and other teenagers in the ghetto by finding them jobs in a big factory, where they worked the night shift making nuts and bolts. "As long as you are working there, you are safe," Leo said. Although the work benefited the German army, Walter didn't mind it because he was doing something he liked. And, he was in love.

The girl's name was Lydia Reindl. She was Walter's age, thirteen, and lived with her parents in the ghetto, which was where they first met. Lydia also worked in the same defense plant as Walter. The two of them would hold hands and sneak quick kisses on the hour-long train ride to and from the factory. In the ghetto, they took long walks together, played Ping-Pong, and talked about how they missed school and the friends who had disappeared. Despite the living conditions in the ghetto, it was a happy time for Walter because he was so smitten with Lydia.

For three months, Walter didn't think much about the

war or the Nazis. All he cared about was Lydia. He loved
the way she flashed her dazzling green eyes at him and
brushed back her silky blond hair. But soon, he noticed,
Lydia started to seem distant and tense. During an
evening stroll, Walter finally asked, "Lydia, is something
wrong?"

She burst out crying. "I can't hold it in any longer,"
she blurted. "My parents made me promise not to tell
anyone, but I have to tell you, Walter. We're going to sneak
out of the ghetto tonight and try to make it to Russia. My
parents say it's our only hope. Walter, I have to go with
them. I want to stay, but they won't let me."

Tears welled up in Walter's eyes. "I don't want you
to go."

Lydia unclasped her necklace, removed a pendant
from it, and gently placed it in Walter's palm. "Would you
keep this as a way of remembering me?"

"I could never forget you, Lydia." He looked at the
words inscribed on the pendant: I LOVE YOU.

Lydia kissed him for the last time and ran off in the
darkness, leaving Walter frozen in grief.

The next morning, Walter rushed to the cubicle where
Lydia and her family lived, hoping maybe they had
changed their minds. But the cubicle was empty — just
like the feeling in his heart. *Will I ever see her again?* Walter
wondered. For days, he tried to stay extra busy, doing
chores, playing with friends, working hard in the factory,
anything to take his mind off Lydia.

Three weeks later, horrible news filtered back to the

ghetto: The Nazis had caught Lydia and her parents during the family's desperate escape attempt and had shot them to death. When word of Lydia's execution reached Walter, he slumped to the ground as if he, too, had been shot. He wept for days.

Up until that moment, Walter had disliked the Nazis but had felt no deeply held hatred for them. Now, he did.

On June 21, 1941, the Nazis announced that everyone in the ghetto was being deported. Loudspeakers began blaring: "Be ready tomorrow morning at seven o'clock. Each person can bring one suitcase. You will be marching down to the train station for resettlement in the east. Be prepared." Although the Jews were upset about leaving their town, they began the preparations. No one knew that the Nazis had built death camps and were beginning mass exterminations.

The next morning, Walter and his family were among the 1,000 Jews who, under armed guard, marched down to an old junkyard, which was next to the train station. They were ordered to file past long tables and hand over any valuables such as necklaces, bracelets, and rings to SS troopers, who were waving pistols and cracking whips. The families were then told to stand in columns. Every so often, Walter would see a Nazi pull a man out of line and drag him into a shed, where he would be beaten and then kicked out, bruised and bloodied. "This is what happens if you try to hide anything!" an officer shouted to the crowd.

As he stood in line, Walter stuck his hand in his pocket and felt the Omega watch his father recently had given him. Walter hadn't turned it over to the Nazis. Suddenly he felt frightened that the watch would be discovered on him. So he dug a hole in the ground with his heel, dropped the watch into the hole, and covered it with dirt. He said to himself, *I'll be back and pick it up later. But I'm not giving up Lydia's pendant. That stays with me in my pocket.*

The Nazis began separating the people in the crowd by age. When a guard pulled Walter out of line, Anny cried out his nickname, "Valti! Valti!" and grabbed her son's arm and hung on to him. An SS officer rushed over and whipped her until she released her grip and fell to the ground, sobbing.

Teenagers, including Walter, fourteen, Edith, eighteen, and their cousin Ilse Borger, fourteen, were put on one train, while middle-aged and older people were herded onto another. As the trains chugged out of the station in different directions, no one on board knew where they were headed.

The train carrying Walter's parents and 900 other Jews stopped briefly in Bedzin, Poland. It just so happened that the chief Jewish representative for that area, Moshe Merin, who was working closely with the Nazis, was standing on the station platform with several members of the Gestapo. The passenger car containing Leo and Anny stopped right in front of them. Merin, a friend of Leo's, glanced at the car and spotted Leo. "Please get that man and his wife off the train," Merin told the officers. A German guard ran into the passenger car and ordered the

Ziffers to get out. Leo and Anny stepped onto the platform just as the train was pulling away. They later learned that the train's final destination was the death camp at Auschwitz, where all those on board were exterminated the next day.

Meanwhile, Walter, Edith, and Ilse were taken to the Dulag, or transition camp, in Sosnowiec in German-occupied Poland. Thanks to Merin's clout with the Nazis, Leo and Anny were transported to the same town, where they were allowed limited freedom. Leo tried to use whatever influence he had left to secure the release of his children and niece.

Every day, the captive young people stood outside at *appell,* while the guards called out names of those who were allowed to leave the Dulag. With each name called, a relieved teenager dashed off. Walter was thrilled when he heard Edith's and Ilse's names. He kept waiting for his to be called. But it never was.

One day, Walter and other teenage boys were put aboard a train and taken away. Hours later, filled with fear, they stumbled off the train in Sakrau, Poland, and marched to a small slave-labor camp surrounded by two ten-foot-tall fences and an electric fence. Certain trusted prisoners, known as *kapos,* or concentration-camp police, acted as guards within the camp. They walked smartly and carried leather whips and seemed not to mind using them. They forced the new prisoners to strip to make sure they weren't hiding jewelry or gold. Then the *kapos* took the prisoners' clothing, sent the prisoners to disinfecting showers, and gave them striped uniforms and round hats to wear.

Giving up his clothes broke Walter's heart, because in his old pants pocket was Lydia's cherished pendant. Like the watch he had hidden in the dirt back in his hometown, he would never see the pendant again.

Walter was put to work shoveling sand from a quarry into a train wagon. Remembering his father's words — "Always do your best" — Walter shoveled hard and fast, filling up his wagon more quickly than his fellow prisoners did. *After all*, he kept reminding himself, *I am somebody*. One afternoon, when he was sweaty and tired but satisfied that he had done a good job, Walter leaned on his shovel. Suddenly, he was attacked from behind and thrown to the ground. As fists slammed into his face and ribs, Walter tried to fend off his attackers, who, to his bewilderment, were his fellow prisoners.

When the flurry of jabs stopped, he wiped the blood off his face and said to them, "I don't understand. Why are you hitting me?"

"You've been here two weeks, and you still haven't learned yet," replied one of his attackers, a prisoner in his twenties who had been in the camp for nearly a year.

"What are you talking about? I'm just doing what they tell me."

"You're doing it too well. You're helping the Nazi cause by working so hard. You've got to do as little as possible, like we do. When the guards watch you, that's when you shovel. When they look away, don't shovel — not unless you want another beating."

Walter nodded. Although he shoveled with less effort, the days of hard labor seemed endless. The prisoners would work for twelve to fourteen hours, in all kinds of weather. Food was scarce — the prisoners generally got a small portion of weak vegetable soup and a small hunk of bread, often stale. Water was scarce, too. Sometimes Walter would be so thirsty he would drink out of a muddy puddle. Many prisoners weren't accustomed to hard physical work and died from cold, heat, hunger, or exhaustion.

The only bright spot for Walter was the occasional letter he received from his parents, who lived with Edith and Ilse in a ghetto in Sosnowiec. Leo had arranged for someone in the town of Sakrau to toss bread over the fence to Walter. It was the only way for a prisoner to get extra food. Most of the care packages the prisoners received from home were intercepted and looted by the guards.

Over the next four years, Walter was shipped from camp to camp, each one more dreadful than the last. With each passing day of his enslavement, he lost a little bit of his identity, of his humanity. To the Nazis he was just another Jewish slave who deserved to die if they couldn't get enough work out of him. He had to constantly remind himself, *I am somebody!* But it wasn't easy.

Walter looked like the rest of the underfed and overworked prisoners — scrawny and weary. Their hair had been cut short, and a swath about one inch wide had been shaved down the middle of each inmate's head, like a reverse Mohawk. That way, prisoners were easily spotted if they tried to escape. Inmates called this haircut *laus allee,* or "lice alley."

Lice were a constant problem for prisoners. They had to delouse themselves every night to prevent the lice from burrowing under the skin and causing infections, which could lead to serious illnesses, such as typhus. Walter would take off his shirt and scrape the seams, where the lice laid their eggs. Then he and fellow prisoners would inspect one another, picking lice out of one another's hair.

The inmates were hungry and malnourished, always trying to find ways to "organize food" — a concentration-camp term for stealing something to eat.

Walter didn't have many friends, because everybody lived for himself. No one wanted to form a close bond with someone who might not be there tomorrow. Many were so sure they would die or be killed soon that they didn't bother tracking the days, the weeks, or the months. Some prisoners turned to suicide, killing themselves by running into the electric fence, rather than live through another day.

But Walter kept believing he would make it. He knew that if he didn't have hope, he wouldn't survive. He refused to think of himself as just another prisoner waiting to die — a *muselmann,* a word used in concentration camps to describe an inmate on the verge of death from starvation or despair. *I am somebody!*

Even so, it was hard to maintain one's dignity as a human being when, for sport, the commandant of a camp would force a prisoner out of the barracks at night and let his German shepherds chase the prisoner and tear him apart. The constant beatings and brutality, the thirst and starvation, the insults and indignities were wearing Walter down. He knew he was losing compassion when he woke up in the barracks one morning and discovered the prisoner next to him was dead. Walter stripped the clothes off the body and put them over his own rags, giving himself a double layer of clothing to ward off the winter cold.

Just when Walter thought it couldn't get any worse, he was sent to the slave-labor camp in Brande, Poland. On Walter's first morning there, he stood at *appell* and watched a scowling Commandant Pompe, the head of the camp, inspect the ranks. Pompe, who walked with a limp because he had a wooden leg, randomly hit a dozen prisoners over the head with his whip. He ordered them to step out and had his guards march them off to the wash barracks.

Minutes later, Walter heard terrible screaming coming from the wash barracks. He wondered what was happening, but he was afraid to ask.

A few days later, while standing at *appell*, Walter was pulled out of line by a guard and taken to a room to meet Peter Gebuehrer, the *kapo* of *kapos*. "Are you the son of Leo Ziffer, the attorney from Cesky Tesin?"

"Yes, sir."

"I know your father. A good man. Assuming you have many of his traits, I have a special job for you. You will be my servant and clean my room and run errands for me. This is a job anyone in camp would kill to have because it comes with extra benefits." Gebuehrer walked over to a big box under a table and kicked it open with his boot. "Take a look at this." It was filled with bread wrapped in packages that had been sent by prisoners' relatives but obviously never delivered to them. "Any time you're hungry, help yourself." Then Gebuehrer opened his closet, which was stocked with preserves and margarine. "However, if I ever catch you eating from this closet," he told Walter, "you will suffer beyond your wildest nightmare."

Suffering is what the camp seemed to specialize in. Most every day at *appell*, Walter saw Pompe select a dozen prisoners, who were marched off to the wash barracks, and then he heard their screams. Finally, Walter got up the nerve to ask Gebuehrer, "What happens to those prisoners?"

"Pray that it never happens to you."

Three weeks later, after another dozen had been led to the wash barracks, guards took Walter and a few other inmates there, and he saw for the first time the fate of the dozen. They had been tortured and killed. On this day, it was Walter's job to pick up the bodies, put them on a cart, and dump them into a grave in the woods. Then he had to wash the blood off the barracks floor. The only reason Walter was able to carry out the orders without sobbing or getting sick was because he had already gotten used to the horrors of concentration camps and had become almost numb to them.

Walter was thankful for the servant job with Gebuehrer because he had more to eat than the other prisoners. But there was no escaping the harsh cruelty inflicted daily on those around him.

One day Walter found himself in the mess hall with Gebuehrer and Commandant Pompe when guards brought in Sam Rabinowicz, a prisoner Walter knew from Cesky Tesin.

Holding up a letter in his hand, Pompe glared at Sam and said, "Did you write this?"

Sam peered through his thick glasses and nodded meekly.

"You tried to smuggle this out, didn't you?"

Knowing he was doomed, Sam puffed out his chest and in a strong voice declared, "Yes. I wanted to tell the world that this is not a slave camp but a death camp and that you —"

The guards started beating Sam with their whips before he could finish his sentence. When Sam's glasses flew off and landed on the floor, Pompe stomped on them. Then the guards dragged Sam off and shoved him in a coal chute. Walter never saw him again.

Walter tried to avoid Pompe at all costs because he knew the commandant was evil and had a hair-trigger temper. One bitterly cold day, while on an errand for Gebuehrer, Walter stopped in the prison boot-repair shop to warm his hands by the fire. His timing couldn't have been worse.

Pompe walked in, saw Walter, and asked, "What are you doing in here?"

"I'm warming my hands, sir. It's cold out there, and my hands are freezing."

Pompe reacted as though Walter had cursed him. "Well," the commandant hissed, "I'm going to warm another part of your body."

Before Walter had time to say anything, three *kapos* grabbed him and Pompe repeatedly lashed him with a whip until he passed out from the pain. As if that wasn't punishment enough — what he had done wrong, Walter didn't know — he had to clean out the smelly sewage in the latrine with a kitchen ladle. It took him two days.

As was the case in all the camps where Walter was imprisoned, no one successfully escaped Brande. The only way out was either to be transferred or to be executed . . . or to die a slow death from hunger, exhaustion, or illness.

Eventually, Walter was transferred to one of the slave-labor camps of Gross-Rosen, in western Poland. Gross-Rosen was the center of an industrial complex and the administrative hub of a vast network of nearly 100 smaller camps that, combined, held more than 70,000 prisoners. Walter laughed to himself when he saw the motto on a sign above the entrance to the camp. He had seen it before at each of the other six camps in which he was held. The sign read "*Arbeit Macht Frei*" ("Work Makes You Free"). Walter chuckled because no prisoner in the camps was *ever* freed for working hard.

After Walter had settled in to his barracks in Gross-Rosen, a prisoner he knew from Sakrau came up to him and said, "Is that you, Walter?"

"Yes, it's me."

"So, you, too, have become a *muselmann*."

Being called that ugly name hurt Walter. Up until then, he had never considered himself anything but a prisoner. Yes, he was skin and bones — he weighed only eighty-seven pounds (thirty-nine kilograms) — but he never thought of himself as a *muselmann*. "I am somebody," he declared. "I am Walter Ziffer."

But he was a different person, both in body and in mind, than the Walter who had arrived at his first slave-labor camp nearly four years earlier. Now eighteen years old, he was numb to the cruelties inflicted on him and his fellow prisoners. He was operating on automatic, doing what he was told as if he were nothing more than a robot.

Every day at Gross-Rosen was the same. Walter and a group of inmates would walk, under heavy guard, through the city of Walbrzych — what the Germans called Waldenburg — and out to a granite quarry. There, they would drill holes in the bedrock, insert dynamite in the holes, and blow up the bedrock.

One winter morning in 1945, as the prisoners were being marched through town, a civilian ran around the corner and threw a wrapped package at them. Shots from the guards rang out. Walter grabbed the package and ripped open the paper. Inside was a thin sandwich with margarine. He managed to tear off a piece of the sandwich and stuff it into his mouth before thirty hands snatched it away from him.

That night, after he returned to the barracks, Walter

took off his shoe and noticed it had a hole in it, and his foot was bleeding. That's when he realized a bullet had grazed his foot, but he hadn't felt it because his toes were so cold.

Walter didn't pay much attention to the wound until three days later, when his foot became badly infected. He hobbled to the prison clinic, where two Dutch doctors told Walter he needed immediate treatment. "We can't let the officers know you are here," said one of the physicians, a prisoner himself. "If they find you, and you aren't able to work, they will kill you."

The doctors hid Walter under a bed and draped a blanket in such a way that it reached all the way to the floor to conceal him. He lay on the floor for several days while they cleaned the wound and fed him bowls of soup. The floor was hard, but it was so much better than working outside in the frigid cold.

The doctors warned Walter whenever an SS officer entered the clinic. More than once while Walter hid, an officer would take a patient out of the clinic and bring him to the main prison, where he and others like him from other nearby camps were lined up along the "death wall" and machine-gunned. Walter remained hidden in the clinic for a week before returning to work.

On the morning of May 8, 1945, Walter was standing at *appell* when he sensed something was different. He looked in the watchtowers. They were empty — and they had never been empty before. But his mind was so drained and deadened that he couldn't make sense of what he was seeing. So he, like all the other prisoners, just stood there, waiting for someone to tell them what to do. He watched as the commandant strolled to the center of the camp, talked to the *kapos*, and walked out of the main gate. Then the commandant took the key chain off his belt, threw it over the fence, and strode off. The *kapos* remained huddled in the center, not doing anything.

"What do you think is happening?" Walter whispered to Emile, a fellow prisoner who stood next to him. "I don't see any guards anywhere."

"I think it's a trap," Emile replied. "They want us to believe that we're free to go, but once we storm out of here, they will machine-gun us."

The prisoners stood still for half an hour, afraid to move. Suddenly, a Soviet army tank roared into view and smashed into the front gate, knocking it down. And still the prisoners stood there for several more minutes.

Finally, Emile nudged Walter and said, "I think it's over. Let's go organize some food."

"We're free. We're really free." Walter didn't shout or jump up and down. He said it matter-of-factly, as though the words had confirmed what he always knew in his heart — that he would survive.

Cautiously, Walter and Emile walked into Walbrzych in search of something to eat. Seeing an abandoned German military truck, they climbed into the back and discovered cans of food. They found a screwdriver and punched holes in the lids, revealing chunks of pork covered in thick white grease. The famished young men each shoveled about a dozen cans' worth of the greasy pork into their hungry mouths. When Walter couldn't stuff another bite into his bloated stomach, he slashed open a sack of sugar, dug his hands in, pulled out a mound, and gobbled it all down. He hadn't eaten meat or sugar for more than four years, and the food tasted fantastic. Suddenly, everything went black, and Walter passed out.

When he woke up, he saw nothing but white. *Am I dead?* he wondered. *Well, if so, I'm not in heaven, because I don't see any angels.* He soon realized he was lying in a bed between two white sheets. When he sat up, he saw a German woman dressed in black standing in the room.

"Where am I?" Walter asked.

"You're in my home," the woman replied. "I saw you and your friend go into the truck, and then I found you both unconscious. A neighbor and I dragged you to my apartment. Apparently, you ate food that you shouldn't have eaten, and ate too much of it, and your body couldn't digest it."

"Why are you helping us?"

"It's all over. We lost the war."

Once they recovered, Walter and Emile decided to organize some clothes and get out of their prison uniforms. They broke into several abandoned homes, where Walter picked out pants, shirts, and a coat — and even an SS officer's raincoat and boots. Worried that a German soldier would come around the corner and shoot them, the two returned to the camp because they didn't know what else to do.

Several days later, women from another prison entered the camp looking for relatives. Walter went up to them and asked, "Did you ever run into a woman named Anny Ziffer?"

"My goodness, yes," said one of them. "She, her daughter, and her niece are in our barracks."

The good news nearly buckled Walter's knees. His heart began pumping so fast he got dizzy. "Where?" he asked the woman.

"About thirty kilometers [eighteen miles] from here. In Langenbielau."

Thrilled by the report of his loved ones' survival, Walter started walking toward their camp as briskly as he could. Early in his trek, he encountered a German army officer on a bicycle. Walter stood in his way and ordered him, "Get off that bike!" The officer obediently dismounted, and Walter hopped on and pedaled toward Langenbielau. Because he was so weak from his imprisonment, Walter didn't get as far as he wanted and had to spend the night in a field. As he gazed up at the stars, which for the first time seemed so bright and sparkly, he said out loud, "I'm free. I'm really free!"

The next day, he arrived at the camp in Langenbielau and went to the women's barracks. He learned that his mother, sister, and cousin were out organizing some food. His whole body tingling with excitement, Walter waited on a bench for their return.

When Walter saw his mother, sister, and cousin enter the barracks a few hours later, tears of unbridled joy trickled down his face for the first time in years. Long-buried emotions of happiness and love began bubbling to the surface as Walter stared ardently at his family. Their heads were shaven, and their bodies were just skin and bones, but they looked beautiful to Walter. He couldn't wait to hug and kiss them. As they neared him, he beamed and was so overcome with emotion that nothing came out of his quivering mouth. The three women glanced at him, smiled — and kept on walking right past him. They went to the far end of the barracks and unloaded their buckets and paper sacks filled with the food they had stolen in town.

Shaking off his disbelief, Walter went up to his mother and said, "Mama, don't you recognize who I am?" With his bald head and paper-thin body, he knew he looked very different from the stocky, dark-haired teenage son she had last seen more than four years ago. "Look in my eyes, Mama. It's me. Valti!"

Suddenly, his mother let out a shriek of pure elation. "Valti! It's really you! I thought you were dead!" Then Edith and Ilse screamed and threw their bony arms around him. All of them wept and held one another tightly as though they were afraid to let go.

"It's incredible!" declared Walter. "We all survived." But then he hesitated. He realized that the only one missing in this touching reunion was his father. "What about Papa? Is he alive?"

"We don't know," Anny replied. "The last we heard he was in Auschwitz."

Walter's heart sank. He knew Auschwitz was the Nazis'

main killing center — a death camp worse than any other. *What are the chances,* he wondered, *that Papa survived?*

Once they had regained their strength, the four headed home, walking 140 miles (225 kilometers) in ten days to Cesky Tesin. As soon as the Ziffers arrived, they received the greatest news of all — Leo was alive! He had reached town a few days earlier and was staying with the family's former live-in cook.

Walter rushed over to the cook's house. He walked in and saw his father sitting in the room, staring at the wall. "Papa," Walter announced. "I'm back! So are Mama and Edith and Ilse!" But Leo kept his eyes glued to the wall and showed no emotion. Puzzled and somewhat scared by his father's behavior, Walter kissed him. Looking into Leo's expressionless eyes, Walter understood that his father was a ruined man, unable to come to grips with the horrors he had seen and ashamed that he had been so wrong about the Germans' treatment of the Jews.

It took several days before Leo began acting more like his old self, talking and smiling and showing affection toward his loved ones. Unfortunately, he was never entirely the same as he had been before the war. But then, what Holocaust victim really was? Leo had lost his faith in humanity, and that had crushed him. Because of the trauma that each member of the family had experienced and their lengthy separation from one another, they were unable to rekindle the same closeness they had shared before the war.

Shortly after the family was reunited, Leo explained

how he had escaped death in the final days of the war: "The Soviet army was close to liberating Auschwitz, so the prison guards ordered us to go on a death march to another camp. I knew I couldn't make it, so I told myself, 'If I'm going to die, I might as well die here.' I sneaked into the laundry room, crawled under a pile of wet laundry, and hid from the German guards. I waited for hours. Then I heard someone speaking in Russian. I crawled out from under the laundry pile — and so did another ten prisoners, like ants out of an ant hole. We were free!"

Leo then said to Walter, "So tell me, Valti, how did you survive?"

"I just knew I would live, Papa," Walter replied. "I wouldn't let the Nazis turn me into something less than human — because I am somebody."

◎

In 1948, Walter kissed his family good-bye and went to America on a student visa. He graduated from high school in Nashville, Tennessee, and later earned an engineering degree from Vanderbilt University. After working for General Motors, Walter obtained a Master's degree in theology and biblical studies at Oberlin College, then earned his Ph.D. at the University of Strasbourg in France and taught biblical studies in that country for several years. He now teaches biblical Hebrew at Mars Hill College in North Carolina. The father of four and grandfather of ten, Walter lives with his wife, Gail, in Weaverville, North Carolina.

Despite Walter's many offers to bring his parents and sister to the United States, they chose to live in Czechoslovakia, in what is today the Czech Republic. His cousin Ilse married a Holocaust survivor and raised a family in Cologne, Germany.

When the Nazis invaded Poland in 1939, five-year-old Sarah Engelberg didn't notice much change in her life in the town of Urzejowice. Her father, Leon, still ran his dairy business, and her mother, Tsivia, still looked after Sarah and her two younger sisters, Miriam, who was three, and Lola, who was one and a half. All of Sarah's energy and attention were focused on getting ready for her first day of school.

For months, Sarah's favorite uncle, Naphtali, had been teaching her how to add and subtract. When she finally walked into her first-grade class, she was eager to show what she knew. Sarah listened attentively to the handsome teacher with the kind smile and twinkling blue eyes.

"Today I'm going to tell you a story about birds," the teacher said to his young students. "There were seven birds that gathered food in a field. Five carried the food to their nests to share with their babies, but two decided to stay in the field and keep eating. Now, who can go to the blackboard and tell this story using math?"

Sarah was the only one who raised her hand. Clad in her prettiest starched dress, she went up to the board and confidently wrote the answer.

$$7 - 5 = 2$$

"That's right," muttered the teacher. But there was no approval in his voice. Instead, his tone was full of disgust and anger that matched the fiery look in his eyes. Sarah was bewildered. This man had seemed so nice just moments earlier. Now he was glaring at her, and she didn't know why. Back home, every time she solved a math problem, Uncle Naphtali would hug her, encourage her, and shower her with praise.

But in the classroom, as she walked back to her desk, Sarah felt an unexplained coldness and a silent bitterness seep into the room, as though what she had written on the board had insulted the entire class. She plopped into her seat and thought, *I don't ever want to come back here.*

When school finished at the end of the day, the teacher again glared at Sarah. He handed her a note and growled, "Give this to your parents."

Sarah hurried home and handed the note to her mother, who read it and told her, "It says that you can't go back to school because you are Jewish, and Jewish children aren't allowed in school."

In a town of about 500 people, of which only fifty were Jews, Sarah was the oldest Jewish child. She was the first to enter school . . . and the first to be expelled. The news crushed her. "But, Mama, I just want to learn. Uncle Naphtali says I'm really smart, and I'm a good learner."

"I know you are," her mother said. "Some day, when the Nazis are forced out of Poland, you'll go back to school and be the brightest student in the class. In the meantime, you can help me take care of your little sisters."

"When will the Nazis leave?"

"Soon, I hope."

But it wasn't soon. For the next three years, the Germans kept a tight grip on western Poland, while the Soviet Union took over eastern Poland. For Sarah that meant no school. She spent her days doing chores and playing with Miriam and Lola in the dirt street in front of their log house, where the girls danced and sang for the neighbors.

In the afternoons, Sarah often visited her next-door neighbor, Tselka Szlywowytz, who was four years older. Because Tselka was Catholic, as were most of the people in the town, she could attend school. So Sarah would stand by her side at the kitchen table and quietly watch Tselka do her homework. Sarah hoped that by being near her friend, she could absorb Tselka's knowledge.

At home, Sarah would hear her parents, aunts, and uncles talk about the German occupation. She didn't understand any of it but could sense something was terribly wrong. She could tell by looking in their eyes and seeing fear and dread. Sarah wanted to ask why they were always wringing their hands and looking sad, but she didn't.

Sarah wasn't afraid of the German soldiers who had arrived in the town, because she never saw them act mean. In fact, they all appeared quite polite, including the three German officers who moved in with the Engelbergs.

Because the town was so small and had no lodging for soldiers, the military simply bunked with local families whether the residents liked it or not. The officers who came to live with the Engelbergs took over the bedroom of Sarah's parents, forcing the couple to sleep in one room with the children. During the day, the officers worked at Nazi headquarters in the town's main square. In the evening, one of the men, Colonel Arnold, would come home early and read the paper until Leon arrived from work. Then the two men would play chess late into the night — they were both good players and evenly matched — and talk endlessly like two old friends. Never once did Sarah see the colonel treat her father with anything other than respect.

And yet . . . she began hearing things, upsetting things, like the rumor that the Nazis were kidnapping Jews and shooting them for no reason at all.

Then there were the edicts, or orders, demanding that all Jews pay more taxes, wear Stars of David, give up their businesses, and turn over all their valuables to the Nazis.

Leon did what the Germans told him to do, but his wife, Tsivia, was defiant. One day, when the Nazi officers weren't around, Sarah overheard her parents arguing, but in a whisper.

"What do you mean you held some jewelry back?" Leon snapped at Tsivia. "We're supposed to turn in all our valuables."

"I'm not giving up my fur coat."

"But what if they find out? We could be shot."

"Don't worry. I wrapped my coat and gave it to Mrs. Szlywowytz for safekeeping."

Around town, Sarah now felt like an outsider. All the others her age, the Christian children, attended school, were free to go anywhere, and didn't have to wear a star or carry papers stamped with a big "J." They all had straight blond hair and blue eyes, and Sarah felt her dark curly hair and brown eyes made her stand out. Sometimes, when Sarah was playing outside, kids called her nasty names, even though all she had done was smile at them.

At home, Sarah noticed that the conversations between Colonel Arnold and her father during their chess games had become more intense. She began seeing a change in her dad. He seemed distracted and anxious. Sarah thought it was because he was still grieving over the death of one of the twin girls her mother had given birth to a few months earlier.

But Leon's anxiety was about more than the death of the baby. In September 1942, shortly after the three Nazi officers left the area, an edict was given to the Jews of the town to assemble at the railroad station the next morning.

Leon announced to the family: "We're not going, and neither should any Jew." Because Jews weren't allowed to gather in groups, Leon spread the word by telling a relative, who told someone else, who told someone else, and so on, until the entire Jewish community got his message.

Sarah's grandfather Aaron Engelberg (Leon's father), a widower who lived nearby, was a deeply religious man who had a great faith in humanity. He tended to defend the Germans and saw no reason to worry. "They are civilized, intelligent, and fair-minded people," Aaron told the family. "They are Christians who will not harm those who don't deserve harm."

Leon shook his head and said, "I have learned from the colonel that this war is different from any other war. I studied his eyes when he spoke. Without ever saying the words, he gave me certain warnings and made me no longer believe the Nazis' assurances that Jews would *not* be harmed. The colonel made it clear to me that our family could *not* survive the war sitting here."

"Don't be ridiculous," scoffed Aaron. "The Germans probably just want to take another census of the Jews and make sure our papers are in order."

"No, they are likely to take us away to our deaths," said Leon. "We must leave tonight. Our lives depend on it."

"You are being a fool, and you are scaring your family."

Sarah, who was in the room during the discussion, broke her silence and sided with her grandfather. "*Tate,*" she said to her father, "please let's not leave. I want to stay. Where will we go? What will we do?"

"We will do what we must. We will live in the fields. Now, go help your mother." The stern expression on her father's face told her that this discussion was over.

As she left the room, she heard Uncle Naphtali, Leon's younger brother, offer to go with the family. "Leon, you need me to help you because of your children. I can carry the little ones."

Leon shook his head. "In case my family and I don't make it, I *insist* that you run off and save your own skin. You'll have a much better chance of surviving without us. We need you to be the one in our family who lives so you can tell the story of what happened to us. When all this ends, and it will, you must tell the world. Do this for us, Naphtali."

Sarah rushed back into the room and hugged her favorite uncle. "I will miss you so much," she said, her lips quivering.

"And I'll miss you," Naphtali said. "But it won't be long before we're together again after the Nazis are defeated. Then we'll read and do math together. Now, be good." He wrapped his arms around Sarah, holding his niece for a long time.

Wiping away her tears, Sarah went into the bedroom and saw that her mother had already packed the children's belongings in bundles.

Shortly after the sun had set, the Engelberg family left the house, not knowing when — or if — they would ever return. Carrying small sacks of their possessions on their backs, Sarah, now eight, and Miriam, six, followed their parents, who were carrying Lola, four and a half, and one-year-old Feige. The Engelbergs were joined by Tsivia's brother, Isaac Gamss; his wife, Leah; their daughters, Sarah, five, and Rachel, four; and son, Nachum, two.

The two families walked quietly into the chilly late-summer evening until they reached a farmer's field, which was dotted with tall haystacks. "We'll spend the night here," said Leon.

"Outside? In the cold?" asked Sarah.

"No, inside these," her father said, pointing to two haystacks. The families dug into the side of each stack and pulled out just enough hay to form a cozy hideaway. Then they crawled inside for the night and covered the hole with hay. It was itchy, but the strong, pleasant aroma had a comforting effect on Sarah.

Still, she wondered why they had to sleep inside a haystack. "Mama, who is living in our house?" she asked her mother.

"No one."

"Then why can't we go live there?"

"It's not safe. The Nazis are looking for us."

"Why can't we stay with our neighbors, like Tselka Szlywowytz?"

"It's now a crime for anyone to assist Jews, so no one is willing to help us. The haystack is our home now. It's safer here."

Because Sarah's father had warned his fellow Jews to flee the town, no Jew — except one — followed the Nazis' orders to show up the next morning at the train station.

The lone Jew was Sarah's grandfather, Aaron, who was put aboard a German train. He would never be seen again. The failure of the rest of the Jews to gather at the station angered the Nazis, and they launched a massive search of the countryside.

For the next three months, as the weather turned colder and damper, the two families hid in haystacks during the day. At night, they searched for food, shaking fruit off trees and pulling vegetables out of gardens. Sarah had never tasted anything as foul as a too-young potato, but she ate it anyway because she was hungry. Sometimes they stole bread. Farmers usually baked bread on Thursdays and stored their loaves on wooden slats in the barn. If the Engelbergs were near, the farmers discovered they had less bread than they thought.

The families were often forced to move from one farm to another. Sometimes it was because a coldhearted farmer discovered them or because the animals needed the hay in the stack. Other times, sympathetic farmers would warn them: "The Nazis are going to search this area. Go to that field over there. It's already been searched." The farmers who were friendly sometimes shared what little food they had. Mostly, they offered the families valuable information about the German soldiers' location.

Sometimes the reports the farmers gave were not good news, like the night a friend approached Leon and Sarah while they were looking for food. "Leon," he said, putting a hand on Leon's shoulder. "I have some terrible news. It's about your brother Naphtali."

Sarah gulped. Her mouth went dry. Part of her wanted to know the truth; part of her wanted to run away so she didn't have to hear what she feared the man was about to reveal.

"The Nazis were searching for Jews. From my farm to the river, they had soldiers every few yards. When they were getting close to Naphtali, he hid in a mud hole by the side of the riverbank and covered himself up. But the leeches began to bite him, so he got out of that hiding place and ran about three hundred meters [one-fifth of a mile] and hid in a haystack. A while later, the soldiers asked one of my farmhands to remove some of the hay, so he took off just a little bit from the top. The Nazis yelled, 'More! More!' and he was forced to keep taking off hay until they found Naphtali."

Tears began welling up in Sarah's eyes. She wanted to cover her ears, but she needed to know the fate of her favorite uncle.

The farmer continued. "Naphtali asked the Nazis to give him a minute so he could be alone with his God. They granted him his wish and then" — his voice began to shake — "they killed him."

Sarah fell to her knees and sobbed. Leon stood motionless, too stunned to cry or utter a moan. Finally, after a minute of silence, he murmured, "But he was supposed to run off days ago. What was he still doing here?"

"He had some milk and bread. He was looking for you, to give you and your family the food."

As Sarah and her father trudged quietly back to their

haystack, she made a promise to herself: *I will survive. I must. When the war is over, I need to be the one to tell people about our family.*

Despite swarms of German soldiers scouring the countryside for Jews, the two families managed to stay hidden. After a time, the children began to creep out of the haystacks and play in the fields, often within sight of farmworkers, who could easily have tipped off the Nazis but instead pretended not to notice the kids. The Engelbergs were lucky, because many other farmers — out of fear for their own safety or because of their anti-Semitism — betrayed Jews who had been hiding in the fields.

Three months of creeping from haystack to haystack and scrounging for food and water had left the families weary and hungry. They worried how they would survive now that winter was fast approaching.

One night, while huddled in a haystack, Sarah heard someone in the field whistle in an unusual way. Her mother gasped and scrambled out of the haystack. Sarah listened as her mother mimicked the whistle, which was immediately answered. Uncle Isaac emerged from his haystack, let loose with the same distinctive whistle, and that, too, was answered.

"Mama, what's happening?" asked Sarah.

"There's only one person who whistles like that — Stanislov Grocholski," Tsivia replied, her voice tingling with glee. Seconds later, a man — Sarah guessed it was Stanislov — appeared and threw open his arms as Tsivia and Isaac rushed to embrace him.

Stanislov had known Tsivia and Isaac since they were children. When he was a teenager, his parents had died from an illness. His aunts and uncles had taken in his younger siblings but figured he and his sister, Kasha, were old enough to fend for themselves. But Tsivia and Isaac's parents, Aaron and Pia Gamss, knew Stanislov and Kasha were too young to be on their own, so they fed and cared for them and made sure they went to school and, because the children were Catholic, went to church. During their early friendship, Stanislov and the Gamss children invented a special way of whistling to one another.

"Someone told me there was a family in the fields living in the haystacks, and the descriptions sounded like 'my Jews,'" Stanislov told Tsivia. "Every night I've been walking in the fields, whistling, trying to find you and Isaac. I jumped for joy when I heard you two whistling back to me."

"You have no idea how happy we were to hear your whistle," Tsivia said.

"I think I can help you," Stanislov said. Despite a Nazi-enforced curfew on everyone in the area, Stanislov came most nights to the haystacks, supplying the families with information and a little food. He was their only link with the outside world, their only friend willing to help them. But it wasn't enough if they were to survive.

"We need shelter for the winter," Tsivia told him one night. "We can't live out here like this. Surely you can find it in your heart to take us in."

"I want to help, but it's too risky. I have my family

to think of first . . . and my wife, Maria, wouldn't stand for it."

"At least ask her."

Stanislov came back the next night and said, "Maria is petrified of the idea. She's afraid the Nazis will kill us if they find out. I wish I could help, but it's impossible."

"I'll make it worth her while," said Tsivia. "I will give her all the jewelry and furs that my sister-in-law and I have, and our money, too."

Two nights later, Stanislov returned. "Okay. My wife is willing to chance it, providing you turn over to her all your valuables . . . particularly your fur coat."

Jubilant, Leon and Tsivia left Sarah and her sisters with Uncle Isaac and Aunt Leah and sneaked back to their town. Their neighbor, Mrs. Szlywowytz, was shocked to see them, because she thought they were all dead. They asked for the fur coat, but she refused, claiming, "You said you'd come back *after* the war and get the coat, but the war isn't over so you can't have the coat."

Tsivia replied, "Listen, if you don't give me the coat, we'll surely die, and if we die, blood will be on your hands. You'll meet your maker and be judged guilty of this great sin."

Mrs. Szlywowytz's eyes widened. "Let me talk to my priest first."

The priest, Father Yanusz, was friends with Leon and knew the Engelberg family, so when Leon and Tsivia returned to Mrs. Szlywowytz's house a few nights later, the coat was ready to go — along with some bread and milk for the children. "Oh," Mrs. Szlywowytz added, "Father Yanusz sends you good wishes."

Late the next night, Sarah, her family, and their five relatives followed Stanislov to his modest log house in the nearby village of Mokrzanka. When they arrived, they quietly climbed a handmade wooden ladder to a trapdoor in the ceiling that opened to his tiny attic. More of a crawl space than an attic, it was only ten feet (three meters) wide and fifteen feet (four and a half meters) long. It felt even smaller under the slanted ceiling, which was only four and a half feet (one and a third meters) high at its peak, too low for an adult to stand up straight. The outside walls on each end were fashioned from weathered wooden slats separated by gaps up to two inches (five centimeters) wide, which let in the chilly night air. The attic didn't have any electricity, plumbing, or furniture.

"Now remember," Stanislov whispered, "no candles, no noise. You must stay as quiet as possible. My wife, Maria, and my children are sleeping. Other than Maria, no one — not even my children — will ever know you are here as long as you don't make any noise. I'll bring you food at night. In the center of the attic are two pails you can use as toilets. I'll empty them every day."

Stanislov's lantern gave off enough light for Sarah to see that the attic was bare except for the pails and the straw that covered the floor. "I'm going to go now," he said. Then he doused the lantern and closed the trapdoor, plunging the families into darkness.

"Let's make the best of it, everyone," said Leon in a hushed voice. "At least it's better than being in the fields."

"How long will we stay here, *Tate*?" Sarah asked.

"Until the danger passes. Maybe a week or two. Maybe a month."

As the two families hunkered down quietly for their first night in the attic, they never imagined how long, how hard, and how tragic their stay there would be.

Sarah's new life was a boring one. At night, they slept on the straw. During the day, they just sat quietly, usually communicating through hand signals or whispers. There was nothing to do, not much to say. They napped often. They couldn't walk around or make any noise, and the children couldn't play. They weren't able to bathe or brush their teeth. The children understood the helplessness of their situation and the anxiety of their parents, so they didn't complain.

The cracks in the walls let into the attic not only slender rays of light but the wind and snow as well. The gaps also acted as narrow windows, so each person had his or her own spot from which to view the world — not that much was ever happening outside. Sarah's vantage point looked out over a field, now barren after the fall harvest. Through the middle of the field ran a lonely country road lined with trees that had shed their leaves. Occasionally a villager in a horse-drawn cart would pass by to ease Sarah's boredom. She spent hours daydreaming, letting her mind take her into the future, where she saw herself all grown up, beautiful, rich, and famous — and eating lots of food.

The big excitement in the attic came when Stanislov opened the trapdoor each night and gave them their daily meal, usually a pot of boiled beans and potatoes. And he'd empty the toilets.

One evening, when winter had sent the wind howling and temperatures plunging, Stanislov told Tsivia and Isaac that he had seen their four other brothers hiding out in a nearby forest.

"You have to bring them here," Tsivia told him. "They'll die out there in this cold."

Stanislov shook his head. "It's too dangerous. If the Nazis see anyone walking after curfew, they'll shoot them."

"But my brothers will freeze. They don't stand a chance out there. At least here in the attic they have half a chance."

"The Nazis will shoot me if I go into the forest, or they'll shoot us all coming back."

"You must try. You can't let them die."

Despite all his protests, Stanislov brought Sarah's four other uncles to the already crowded attic. A crawl space in which no adult could stand up now was crammed with fifteen people — seven children and eight adults.

The winter was cruel. Snow and bitter wind blew through the cracks and swirled around inside the attic as the families huddled together, trying to stay warm. Some mornings Sarah would wake up covered in snow and see the rest of the snow-covered, sleeping clan looking like giant sugarcoated pastries.

It soon became clear that Sarah's baby sister, Feige, was getting weaker and wouldn't be able to survive much longer.

She was skin and bones and had a big belly — signs of malnutrition. She bawled often, forcing her mother to muffle the cries by putting her hand over Feige's mouth and rocking her. Feige was too young to understand how her crying put the others in danger.

One morning, Sarah woke up and noticed her parents' eyes were red and puffy, their faces streaked with tears. Something was wrong. She scanned the attic to see if everyone was all right, looking at her uncles, aunt, cousins, parents, sisters . . . *Oh, no! Feige is gone!*

"Mama," Sarah whispered, "where is Feige?"

Tsivia shook her head, put her finger to her lips — a signal not to talk about this anymore — and then buried her head in her hands.

Did Feige die? Did they take her someplace during the night? Sarah wanted to ask but she couldn't. She didn't know what had happened to Feige, but whatever it was, she didn't think she'd ever see her baby sister again.

Tsivia remained depressed from that moment on. She would sit in the corner and silently shed tears every day for the infant she could no longer cradle in her arms. She wouldn't talk about Feige, and neither would Leon. They each suffered separately and never shared the pain, hoping to spare Sarah and her sisters the truth. But the girls hurt, too. They just never could express it and suffered in silence like their parents.

Summer in the attic was as unbearable as the winter — except that now it was so hot and stifling, the stuffy environment sapped everyone's will to go on living. There was no running water in the house. Sarah and the other kids would lie by the cracks in the wall, hoping to catch a whiff of breeze, their parched mouths open, begging for water. "I don't care about food," Sarah whispered. "Just water." Then her imagination would carry her off to a sparkling, cool mountain lake, where she splashed and played and guzzled gallons of refreshing water.

By now, the families had been holed up in the attic for nine months, and there was still no end in sight. There was nothing they could do but continue to wait, knowing their fate rested in the hands of Stanislov and his wife, Maria. But tension was building for the couple after they heard reports of Nazis murdering Poles who hid Jews.

One boiling hot afternoon, while gazing through her "window," Sarah saw Maria outside feeding her chickens. "You miserable creatures!" Maria shouted. "You are nothing but trouble. One of these days, I'm going to put poison in your food and get rid of all of you!" Maria then turned toward the attic and glared. "Miserable creatures!"

Sarah bolted upright. *Oh, my gosh!* she thought. *She's talking about us!*

The others in the attic heard Maria, too, and knew exactly what she meant: She wanted the Jews in her attic to leave *now.* But they had no intention of moving out. Later that night, one of Tsivia's brothers, Mordechai, confronted Stanislov about Maria's threats.

"She is sick with worry," Stanislov explained. "Sick in the head from fear."

"I shouldn't have to remind you that my parents took

care of you and your sister, or that it's your duty as Christians to help us survive," Mordechai told him. "And I shouldn't have to remind you of the jewelry, money, and fur that our families gave you for your troubles."

"But Maria is scared. I am, too."

"We all are, Stanislov. That's what war does to people."

No more was said about leaving. The days and nights dragged on and on. A year had passed, and now they were dealing with another winter in the frigid attic, where they shivered and ached. For weeks, Sarah's little cousin Nachum had no appetite and wasn't eating. All he did was sleep. And then, one dreary, cold morning, he didn't wake up. His body had wasted away until there was nothing more to waste.

Nachum's death devastated his mother, Leah, who was ill herself. Sarah could tell that her grief-stricken aunt had lost faith because she always stared vacantly into space, mumbled to herself, and stopped eating. Sarah knew it was just a matter of time before Leah gave up. On a Friday night, while sitting on the straw, Leah looked at everyone — not as a group but individually — as if her sad, dark eyes were saying good-bye to each person. When she was done, Leah lay down on the straw and stopped breathing.

As he had done with Nachum, Stanislov gently took Leah's body, wrapped it up, and buried it in the field.

And now there were only twelve left.

Nachum's and Leah's deaths brought the mood in the attic to a new level of despair. Day after day, the survivors sat glum-faced, wondering who was going to die next.

As winter turned into spring, Sarah grew increasingly worried. Her parents — the ones she had counted on to protect her and her sisters through this miserable war — were coming apart emotionally. Her mother seldom spoke but continued to cry and pine for Feige.

Sarah's father — a man who had been like a rock for Sarah — was teetering on the brink of hopelessness. "I don't think I'm going to make it," he whispered to Sarah. "If I should die, you must take care of your mother and sisters."

"Don't talk like that, *Tate*. You're going to survive. We all are."

"Sarah, you just turned ten. You are strong and smart for your age. You can handle the responsibility."

"You're not going to die!" Sarah said, more loudly than she should, causing the others to shush her.

Sarah didn't want to think about death or her parents or the attic. She didn't want to think about anything. She crept over to her little crack in the wall and gazed out at the countryside. It was a sunny but cold day and exceptionally bright, because a late-season snowfall had blanketed the area and was reflecting the sun's rays. Her mind had begun to drift when she spotted three figures — farmers, she assumed — plodding through the snow toward the house. *It must be nice to be able to walk in the sunshine,* she thought. *I wonder who they are?* Then she noticed the uniforms and the rifles slung over their backs. *They aren't farmers. They're German soldiers!*

"*Tate! Tate!*" she said in a loud whisper. "Nazis! They're coming here!"

"Everybody stay perfectly still," Leon ordered.

Moments later, the soldiers arrived at the house and talked to Maria, who was alone. For the next ten minutes, the families sat like statues, knowing that a cough, a sneeze, or the shifting of their feet could alert the soldiers, who were standing directly below them. Sarah was so terrified that she could hardly breathe. *Is Maria going to give us away? If they find us, they'll kill us. What if Miriam and Lola start squirming?* She looked at her frightened sisters, who were clutching her father, not moving. *Are the soldiers looking for us? Oh, Maria, please, please, please don't squeal on us.*

Sarah's eyes stayed focused on the trapdoor, knowing that if it opened, Maria had tipped off the soldiers. If that happened, Sarah would have only minutes, perhaps seconds, left to live. *Please don't open. Please don't open.*

Finally, the German voices began to fade. But no one in the attic moved, because there was no guarantee that all the soldiers had left. Maybe one had stayed behind. So for the rest of the afternoon, the families remained frozen. Not until later that night, when Stanislov arrived with their dinner, did they relax.

"Maria told me that three Nazi soldiers came by today, but she doesn't understand German and they didn't speak Polish," Stanislov explained. "They kept pointing to the road and the snow, and finally they got fed up and left."

Soon another summer arrived, which meant the families were nearing the end of their second year hidden in the attic. No one had ever thought they would be stuck up there for so long — or that they could have lasted under such awful conditions.

Around this time, Sarah began to notice a shift in the mood of the adults. It seemed more upbeat, although she wasn't sure why. She thought the change had something to do with the newspaper that Stanislov often brought to Leon, who would sit by a crack in the wall for light and read every word before passing it on to his brothers-in-law. The local Polish paper published only stories the Nazis approved. One day an article stated that the Germans had "invaded" a certain town, but Leon knew his geography. The town was located *behind* German lines. "That was no invasion," he told the others. "It was a retreat. The Nazis are pulling back." And then he cracked a smile that Sarah hadn't seen in months.

Every day after that, over the next several months, Sarah studied her father as he read the paper, waiting for that special moment when he would grin, because it meant the Germans were being pushed out of Poland. Leon was smiling more frequently. Sarah's hopes of liberation — of being free once again — began to soar.

Then, one day in the fall of 1944, the family heard shooting in the distance. Although they couldn't see anything, they could tell by the sounds that it was a fierce firefight. "The Germans must be fighting the Russians," said Leon. The battle raged through the day and into the night. And then came silence. No one in the attic knew what had happened, because Stanislov and his family, like all the other villagers, had fled their home when the shooting started. The village remained eerily quiet, and before falling asleep, Sarah wondered what the morning would bring — good news or bad news.

She was already awake when the trapdoor began to creak open the next morning. For a split second, Sarah thought the Nazis were about to enter, and she instinctively backed away. Her tense body relaxed when she saw it was Stanislov.

"You are free," he announced. "You can go home now."

At first, no one said a word or even moved, as though they didn't believe what they had just heard. And they couldn't understand why Stanislov was shouting. Actually, he was speaking in a normal voice, but because they hadn't heard someone talk in anything above a whisper for two years, it sounded to them like he was shouting.

"The Russians have driven out the Germans, and you are liberated," Stanislov said. He wondered why these people weren't reacting to the joyous news they had been yearning for since the day they arrived.

Like their bodies, the minds of the family in the attic had been confined for such a lengthy period, it was hard for them to respond. They were in shock. They had been concealed in a crawl space for so long, it was difficult to suddenly accept that they were free. But as the minutes passed and the words "you are liberated" sank in, smiles spread across their faces.

For Sarah, it seemed like a dream almost too good to be true. Her only wish had finally been realized. She could go home again.

But two years of being cooped up in a cramped attic, unable to use everyday muscles, had taken a terrible toll on the survivors. Their legs didn't work well, so Stanislov had to help them by guiding their feet onto each rung of the ladder as they slowly made their way to the ground floor.

Once all of them were down, they took turns shaking Stanislov's hand and thanking him. Because their shock hadn't worn off yet, their gratitude was reserved.

Although the Nazis had been beaten, Stanislov was still cautious. "You must leave now and never tell a soul who hid you," he said to the survivors. "It must remain our little secret forever."

He opened the front door, and for the first time in two years, Sarah stepped out into the world. As much as she had imagined what a glorious day this would be — and it *was* glorious — she hadn't counted on the consequences of living like statues in a darkened room for so long. The summer sun blinded everyone, forcing them to cover their eyes. Their legs, weak from so little use, wobbled with each unsure step. When anyone tried to talk in a normal voice, their words came out in squeaks.

To the local farmers, the twelve survivors were quite a sight — a dozen pasty-white grown-ups and children crawling and staggering slowly along the road. But they were like thousands of other survivors throughout Europe who were coming out of hiding and making their way back to the world of the living, back to their homes.

Late in the day, the group arrived in their town of Urzejowice. Sarah's heart began to pound as she neared the house she had left so long ago. She let out a yelp when she caught her first glimpse of the only home she had ever known. She wanted to run, but her scrawny legs were too tired from the all-day hike.

Her joy was tempered once she went inside, because absolutely nothing, not one piece of furniture, was left. The Engelbergs soon learned that after they had abandoned their house, it had been taken over by people who had lost their home in a big city and needed shelter. These refugees had broken up all the furniture and used it as kindling to warm themselves during the winter. But although the house was now empty, it was still home — the Engelbergs' home.

Upon their return, Sarah learned the sad truth about her sister Feige. When the baby became seriously ill, her parents had decided to take her out of the attic. Risking death if the Nazis caught them, they had walked nine miles (fifteen kilometers) that night, back to Urzejowice, where they had wrapped the baby in a blanket and placed her on the steps of the Catholic church, in the hope that Father Yanusz or someone else would find her and care for her. Then, with their hearts broken, Leon and Tsivia had rushed back to the attic, arriving just before dawn. But what they now found out was that Feige had been too sick and had died soon after she had been left on the church steps.

Despite the death of her baby sister, Sarah expected to go back to her old life and see her old friends. *Wait until I tell them what we went through,* she said to herself. *They won't believe we lived through such an experience.* But during those first few weeks back, Sarah, like the rest of her family, had little knowledge of the Nazi death camps or of the millions of Jews who had been murdered.

Sarah waited for her Jewish friends and relatives to return. But none ever did. Hers was the only Jewish family from the town to survive.

For Sarah, there was no one left to tell.

The Engelbergs left Poland and in 1947 arrived in the United States, where they settled in New York City. To seem more American, Sarah changed her name to Sally — in honor of her favorite aunt — and chose not to talk about her Polish past because, as one of her uncles told her, "If you're not chained to your memories, you can build a new life." Sally attended City College, earned a master's degree in education, and became a high school teacher. She married Ken Frishberg and raised two children.

When Sally's son was seven years old, he asked her questions about Jewish history. It was then that Sally decided to tell her children — and anyone else who would listen — the whole truth about her family history. In 1986, accompanied by her children and several relatives, Sally returned to Poland to face her past. (Her sisters, Miriam and Lola, declined to go, believing it would be too painful for them.) Sally showed the younger gen-

eration her former town, her house, the fields where the family took cover — and the attic of the Grocholski home.

Although Stanislov had died years earlier, his wife, Maria, still lived there and greeted Sally warmly. Maria apologized for her behavior during the war, admitting, "I was in a bad state of mind." Maria's children told Sally that they remembered hearing voices in the attic during the war, but when they asked their father about the sounds, he ordered them never to mention what they had heard again. No Jews have lived in the town since the Engelbergs left.

During Sally's visit, a youngster rode his bicycle by her group and shouted, "Heil Hitler!" The next day they found a swastika painted on the side of her old house — proof that the curse of anti-Semitism had been passed down to a new generation.

Nevertheless, visiting the attic helped ease the secret hurt that Sally had buried in her heart, and it gave strength and inspiration to her son, daughter, relatives — especially her niece Debbie Goodstein, who made an award-winning documentary of the trip called Voices from the Attic.

Sally volunteers as a docent at the Museum of Jewish Heritage in New York City.

Mathei Jackel could barely breathe or move. He was crammed with eighty other prisoners into a hot, steamy boxcar that normally would hold no more than thirty people. The stench from the sweat of prisoners — bewildered and frightened men, women, and children, many sick and dying — made Mathei want to throw up.

The ten-year-old boy pressed his nose against a crack in the wooden wall, trying desperately to catch a whiff of fresh air. The train clacked slowly through the Romanian countryside, its dozens of boxcars overstuffed with Jewish people who, like Mathei, were wondering what horrible fate awaited them at the end of the line.

Mathei was once a happy-go-lucky boy growing up in a Jewish home in Timisoara, Romania, with his father,

Bernhard, a traveling salesman; his mother, Josefine, a housewife; and his younger brother and an infant sister. Mathei was a bright boy who spoke three languages — German at home, Hungarian on the street, and Romanian at school. He played and studied with kids from different ethnic backgrounds and always felt that he fit in. But Mathei learned otherwise after Germany took control of Romania in the fall of 1940 and forced the Romanian army to join the Nazis.

Some older school friends invited Mathei to a park, where they dared him to join them in a pond. Once he jumped into the water, they surrounded him and shouted, "You little Jew, now you will never get out of here alive!" They pounced on him, and began beating him and shoving him under the surface. Although he was only seven years old, Mathei fought back furiously and managed to escape. Bleeding, bruised, and wet, he ran home and wept, not from the pain of his injuries but from the hurt in his heart. The children he had thought were his friends had turned on him for no reason other than his faith. His parents transferred Mathei to a *heder*, a Jewish religious school. But even so, some of his non-Jewish former schoolmates would chase him on the street and call him "dirty Jew."

Meanwhile, German tanks like the deadly Panzer III and the powerful Tiger thundered down the streets. The Nazis painted the Star of David on the houses where Jews lived and made them wear the yellow Star of David on their clothes. Mathei wore such a star on his back and another on his chest.

Then, one horrible day, the Germans barged into Mathei's house and dragged his father away. That was the last time the family ever saw Bernhard. Mathei's mother knew it was only a matter of time before the Germans came for her sons. So she arranged for her younger son to move in with an aunt near Timisoara and sent Mathei to live with her Christian friend Mrs. Schaechter, whose husband had been killed in the war. Mrs. Schaechter — who had a daughter, Oronka, about Mathei's age — treated Mathei like her own son, except he had to continue wearing the yellow star whenever he went outside because it was the law. Mrs. Schaechter and Oronka taught Mathei to knit, and the three of them spent their time knitting caps, gloves, and scarves. In the evenings, they played card games by candlelight.

In the summer of 1944, just before his tenth birthday, Mathei went with two Christian friends to the town of Arad, about thirty miles (forty-eight kilometers) away. They were roaming through the outdoor market when suddenly a German army truck pulled up behind them. "It's an *aktzia*!" they shouted. Mathei was easily spotted — he was wearing the star — and was captured before he could flee. The soldiers threw him into the canvas-covered back of a truck, which was already filled with more than two dozen other terrified children.

The truck drove straight from the market to the train station, where Mathei joined hundreds of other Jews of all ages who had been rounded up in the latest *aktzia*. After the soldiers shoved them into cramped boxcars and locked the doors, the train slowly lurched out of the station. None of the prisoners knew where they were going. All Mathei knew was that the train was heading north.

⊚   ⊚   ⊚

And now here he was in this stinking, stuffed boxcar, the stench of death and misery all around him. Mathei's weakening legs ached, but there was no room to sit down. His empty stomach growled, but there was no more food for the passengers. His parched throat hurt, but there was no water. How long had he been suffering like this? He'd lost count of the days. He, like each of the other prisoners, had been given a loaf of bread to eat for the trip. That was their only food. But Mathei had finished eating his by the end of the second day. And that had been days ago.

While people pushed and jostled one another, Mathei held his ground so he could stay near the door of the boxcar. That way he could breathe in fresh air through the crack between the wall and the door. Also, he refused to move because he had a feeling it was important for him to remain at that spot.

No one talked much. Most were lost in their own thoughts. All Mathei could think about was water. In the stifling heat of that packed boxcar, he was tormented by thirst. But there was no hope of getting a drink.

The train traveled ever so slowly, stopping for hours at a time. Every once in a while, the doors would open and soldiers would drag out the bodies of the old and the sick who had given up.

For every corpse that was removed, the Nazis shoved a

new prisoner in its place, so that the boxcars remained cruelly overloaded. Each stop brought more information from the new prisoners. After a stop in Hungary, Mathei overheard the Hungarian Jews talking about extermination camps: "We are heading to our doom."

The Jews from Romania, who had been on the train for days, believed that everyone on board was being sent to a work camp. "I refuse to believe that we, all innocent people, are going to be murdered," said one Romanian. Added another, "Our only hope is that we obey the Germans or else they will kill us." Said a third, "They can't murder an entire race of people."

Mathei wanted to believe what they said, wanted to believe that the Nazis wouldn't kill Jews simply for being Jewish, wanted to believe, like so many others on the train, that the Jews were being moved, or "resettled," to a new area.

Later, in Czechoslovakia, the train stopped again. More dead were taken off, and new prisoners were pushed into the boxcars. But these Jews had information that caused a new level of panic among the rest of the passengers. The new arrivals had received word that the train was going to an extermination camp in Poland, probably Auschwitz, which wasn't far away. "They gas people there, including women and children," said one of the Czechs. "Then they burn the bodies. That's what awaits all of us."

By now, many in the boxcar were murmuring about an escape attempt. But others still clung to the hope that they would soon be arriving at a work camp and not a death camp. Mathei no longer believed that.

When he heard the Czechs talk about children being gassed, he wanted to throw up, but he had nothing in his stomach. However, what he did have was a burning desire to live. *I have to escape*, he told himself. *Maybe I'll die trying, but it's better than just letting them kill me.* He felt lucky that he was standing next to the door. It meant he had a chance — although a very slim one — to break out.

The next night, the train stopped at a water tower outside the town of Bielsko-Biala in southern Poland. "We're close to Auschwitz," whispered a Czech to those around him. "I say we make a run for it. It's now or never."

With his heart pounding wildly, Mathei muttered a quick prayer to himself and prepared to flee. Or die.

When the soldiers opened the door to the boxcar to remove the dead bodies, a dozen people burst outside into the uncertain darkness. Mathei was one of the first. The escapees ran in every direction as the startled soldiers shouted at them to halt and began shooting.

Mathei crawled under the train and emerged on the opposite side from where the soldiers were firing. He made a mad dash into the woods and toward the mountains. Weak from hunger and thirst, Mathei kept running in the blackness, stumbling and falling over roots, rocks, and streams. He kept running until he could no longer hear the gunfire. Then he ran some more before collapsing in a heap, cold and wet, in a shallow cave. He fell fast asleep.

Early the next morning, a friendly villager found Mathei sprawled out on the ground. The man gave him something to eat and drink and then, claiming it wasn't safe to remain there, led him higher up the wooded mountain.

After they reached a clearing in the forest, the man sat Mathei down under a tree and left, saying help would arrive soon. Mathei wondered if he should trust the man but then thought, *What choice do I have?* The sun was coming up and began taking the chill out of the air. *It feels so good to be far from that awful train. I wish I could stay. . . .*

Suddenly, a tall blond man in his early twenties, wearing a torn German army uniform, appeared. Mathei jerked to his feet, his eyes wide with dread, fearful that a Nazi had found him and would now kill him. Speaking in German, the man peppered the boy with questions. After Mathei told the stranger about the *aktzia*, the train, and the escape, the man said, "My name is Hans, and I'm from Austria. I enlisted in the German army, but when I found out what the Nazis were doing to the Jews, it turned my stomach. I knew I could never be a part of something so horrendous, so I became a deserter. Now I'm a leader of a group of forty Partisans."

Mathei had heard of the Partisans. Wearing stolen German uniforms or just plain street clothes, these soldiers were part of the Polish underground — the resistance fighters of Nazi-occupied Poland. Fathers, grandfathers, and young boys fought side by side with only red-and-white armbands for identification. The Partisans came from different countries: Jews from the Soviet Union who had served in the Red (Soviet) Army; Hungarian,

Romanian, and Polish prisoner-of-war escapees; German army defectors; and others who shared a common hatred of the Nazis.

The Partisans, who communicated among themselves in German, operated mainly in the forests and mountains of southern Poland. From their hideouts, they made raids against the German rear lines, gathering intelligence about troop movements, blowing up bridges, derailing trains, slashing telephone and telegraph lines, pouncing upon small enemy forces, and setting fire to supply depots. The Partisans fought with whatever weapons they could lay their hands on. They hurled handmade Molotov cocktails — flaming bottles of gasoline — at trucks. They raided German convoys and supply dumps, and scavenged weapons from battlefields. Stealth, deception, and surprise were the hallmarks of their operations. Enemy motorcyclists were toppled by wire strung across the road. German tanks hiding in the woods sometimes erupted in flames when the Partisans set fire to the trees. And, occasionally, enemy vehicles rumbled over a bridge just as it collapsed because the Partisans had sawed through the beams below.

"The Germans reserve a special hatred for us Partisans," Hans told Mathei. "Those comrades who are captured face a fate worse than death. If you are caught, you will be tortured. Then they will shoot you or hang you."

Mathei gulped. But he didn't want to show any fear.

"So," said Hans, "would you like to be one of us?"

Mathei nodded and declared, "I am a Partisan now!"

Hans laughed. "Well, young Partisan, I think we need to put some meat on your bones. Come with me. Let's get you some food."

"We don't have to walk too far, do we? I'm still pretty weak."

Hans laughed again. "No, it's not too far."

Only then did Mathei realize that the clearing in the forest actually was the main camp of the Partisans. They had built bunkers about nine feet deep, with trenches going from one to the other and also leading out into the forest. These bunkers and trenches were so skillfully made and camouflaged with sticks and leaves that the enemy could be walking right by them and not know it. Some of the bunkers were for sleeping, and others contained weapons and explosives. Still other bunkers held the Partisans' food supply, which consisted mostly of potatoes, eggs, butter, tea, sugar, and conserves of meat. The meat tins were stolen from the German army. Some of the food originally came from the American army. It had been commandeered by the Germans before the Partisans stole it for their own use.

Nearby were mineral springs, where the Partisans took drinking water. They washed themselves in hot springs, although Mathei couldn't understand why they were called "hot" because the water was pretty cold.

While Mathei was resting and building his strength during his first week with the group, he learned from the Romanian Partisans in the camp just how brutal the Nazis were to the Jews in his own country. Half of the 320,000

Jews living in the regions of Bessarabia, Bukovina, and Dorohoi had been murdered. Jewish homes and businesses had been looted by local Nazi sympathizers, often just minutes after the Jews were taken away. Tens of thousands of Jews had been machine-gunned in the forests. In Bucharest, Romania's capital city, the Nazi-backed Iron Guard terrorized Jews while the Jews chanted religious hymns.

As he listened to these ghastly stories, Mathei wondered if his father had suffered a similar fate. Was his brother safe? His baby sister? His mother? He blotted those thoughts out of his mind. *No, I don't have time to think about them. I am a Partisan now.*

Hans became like a father to Mathei. So did Boris, a Jew from the Soviet Union who had been a *kommissar*, or officer, in the Red Army. The men cared for him, taught him, and encouraged him. Boris was concerned about Mathei's health. "You must eat all your food," Boris would tell him, "because you never know when you'll get your next meal." Hans made sure that Mathei was warm and dry when they went to sleep in the bunkers.

The Partisans had given Mathei a revolver to protect himself and taught him how to shoot it. Once Mathei mastered the revolver, he graduated to a submachine gun called a Schmeisser. With the Schmeisser, Mathei could fire as fast as his trigger finger could squeeze a round. He wore a long coat that had a hole in it. He'd keep his Schmeisser hidden under the coat and then shoot out of the hole.

Operating in the Beskids Mountains — a range between Poland and Czechoslovakia — the Partisans trained Mathei to be a scout. The members of the group brought Mathei to different villages to collect intelligence. They would place him with a local family friendly to the Partisans, where he would stay for several days, posing as a relative or a war orphan. Meanwhile, the head of the family would take Mathei on a bicycle tour of the village that Mathei was to spy on.

He kept track of people coming and going and identified those villagers who were working with the Germans. Mathei would report back whenever he saw German soldiers deliver food to any family in the village. Then the Partisans would confront that family and seize all the supplies for themselves.

Mathei was soon taking part in major military actions, carrying dangerous explosives, such as TNT, on his back. The Partisans would use the explosives to blow up railroad tracks and bridges, disrupting the Nazi supply lines.

During one mission, Mathei helped place sticks of dynamite under a bridge, lit the fifty-yard-long (forty-five-meter-long) fuse, and ran behind a boulder. An enormous blast echoed off the mountains, drowning out the cheers of Mathei and his fellow Partisans as the structure collapsed into the river.

When Mathei returned to camp, Hans greeted him warmly. "Good job," he said. "Here, I want to show you something." Hans was holding a piece of paper, a warning that a top Nazi officer had issued to his troops. "We found it after we ambushed a platoon of Nazis," said Hans.

"They're afraid of us and know they can't stop us." The warning was written to the soldiers, reminding them that the Partisans liked to strike when the Nazis least suspected it, especially when there was no fighting going on. Hans read a passage from the warning to Mathei: "We Germans make the mistake of thinking that if neither offensive nor defensive operations are in progress, then there is no war at all. But the war is going on . . . when we are cooking potatoes, when we lie down to sleep. A soldier must carry his weapon always and everywhere."

Life for the Partisans in the mountain forest was difficult, especially in the winter, when it was cold and wet. They often had to move from place to place to avoid being discovered by the German soldiers, leaving much of their gear and equipment in the bunkers. Mathei trudged through snow and survived by raiding farmers' food supplies and eating berries. Sometimes he and his group received help from local villagers, but the Partisans couldn't count on much assistance because of people's fears of the Nazis. Besides, the Partisans lived in constant danger of local informers revealing their whereabouts to the Germans, so the fewer people they associated with, the better.

Many times, the Germans encircled the forest with tanks and armored vehicles filled with soldiers. Then they would firebomb the forest, trying to flush out the Partisans. But Mathei and his group always managed to escape by spreading out and firing their weapons from all directions to confuse the soldiers, then hiding in their secret bunkers.

It was a difficult and scary life for Mathei. At an age

when he should have been playing soccer and attending school, Mathei was conducting spy missions, stealing food, and blowing up bridges. For a year, this now grown-up ten-year-old had done everything — and more — that had been asked of him. But he balked when it came time for "the test."

Mathei faced "the test" when the war was nearing an end. The Soviet army had the German soldiers on the run in Poland, fleeing back toward Germany.

Mathei had just completed a spy mission in which he had identified a family who had been helping the Nazis. He and five Partisans entered the house to confront the family. A girl of about eighteen years old was the only one home.

"You are a disgrace!" the leader of the group of Partisans hissed at her, spitting on the floor. "You are nothing but swine!"

Mathei stood next to the leader while the other Partisans gathered the family's food supplies to take back to their camp.

Unexpectedly, the leader turned to Mathei and ordered, "Take out your gun."

Mathei did as he was told.

"I am going to give you a test to see if you are a man. Shoot her!" the leader commanded.

Mathei froze. Sure, he had fired his weapon many times in the past. But it was usually in self-defense or to lure Nazi soldiers toward him and into a Partisan ambush.

He had never actually executed someone. Despite all the horror Mathei had witnessed, the heartache he had felt, and the agony he had endured throughout this terrible war, he still knew right from wrong.

"I-I c-can't," Mathei stammered.

"She doesn't deserve to live," the leader said. "She helped the Nazis, which makes her a Nazi. If you're a man, you will kill her now."

Tears welled up in the terror-stricken blue eyes of the trembling girl. She didn't say a word. She didn't have to. Mathei could tell by the look on her face that she was silently pleading with him, begging him, to spare her.

"Mathei, she is our sworn enemy. She is a Nazi. Think of the millions of Jews who have been gassed and butchered and burned. Think of the millions of Jews who are living skeletons in the concentration camps. This is your chance for revenge. Now, be a man and shoot her!"

Mathei had stolen from villagers, shot at soldiers, and blown up bridges — all for a just cause. But this? This would be murder.

"If you don't do what I tell you, you will not get any food. Shoot her!"

Mathei wished he could be anywhere else but right here, right now. He was not even eleven years old. He wasn't prepared to face this kind of moral dilemma. *I'm just a kid, and I don't deserve any of this.* The more he thought about it, the angrier and more frustrated he became. He was here because the world had gone crazy, bloodthirsty, mad.

Against Jews. *Why was I born a Jew? None of this would have happened to me if I hadn't been born a Jew.* Mathei stared at the girl but didn't really see her. And as hurtful images flashed in his mind — his schoolmates beating him up in the pond, the soldiers dragging away his father, the train heading to the death camp — Mathei raised his pistol and aimed it at the girl.

Then he closed his eyes and pulled the trigger.

The earsplitting bang still ringing in his ears, Mathei dashed blindly out of the house, past his fellow Partisans, past the villagers milling in the street. He ran and ran deep into the woods, feeling an anguish in his heart that he had never felt before. *I'm just a kid.*

No one said anything to Mathei about that day. And he never said anything about it to the other Partisans, either, so he never found out what happened to the girl. But he noticed a change in himself. He seemed more numb to the pain of all that he had endured, and he felt a certain coldness creep into his soul.

This numbness was the only way he could function, especially now, as the war wound down and he and his fellow Partisans would find abandoned boxcars filled with dead prisoners. They would gently and silently place the bodies in mule-drawn wagons and take them higher up in the mountains, where they would bury the remains in mass graves. Sometimes Mathei buried members of his own Partisan group who yearned so much for revenge that they took too many risks and paid the ultimate price. But never once did he bury any of the German soldiers whose bodies littered the forests.

And then one day it was over. The Nazis had lost. On a warm summer day in 1945, Hans, Boris, and the rest of the Partisans bid Mathei and one another farewell and went their separate ways.

Mathei, who had just turned eleven, was on his own. His only possessions were a knapsack with a few clothes, a long coat, and his Schmeisser. Soon, he hooked up with a couple of teenage Partisans and roamed the region. They were vagabonds who had thought only of survival for so long that they had forgotten how to live like normal children.

Their life centered on two objectives: finding something to eat and finding a place to sleep. During the day, the boys would steal food at the local market, and at night they would hop into the boxcar of a freight train and go to sleep. They didn't care where the train was heading. They were child hoboes.

Mathei didn't want to return to Romania; it held too many painful memories. Everyone and everything he loved in his homeland had been taken from him. He didn't want to be close with anyone, not even his family, because experience had taught him that human beings were more threatening than any animal that might be roaming in the forests. For the next year, all that mattered to him were sleep and food.

Then, in the summer of 1946, Mathei met several

shlichim, representatives for a future new country for Jews. They were touring the region, looking for homeless children so they could offer them a chance at a better life.

Mathei was suspicious of these representatives at first, but eventually he agreed to listen to what they had to say. When a group leader of the *shlichim* realized Mathei was hiding a Schmeisser under his coat, he convinced the boy to give him the weapon. "That's not something a twelve-year-old should have. You're still a child."

Indeed, after watching other children play, Mathei wanted nothing more than to be a child again. But it wasn't easy. The war had made him older than his true age. He had seen too much horror, encountered too much sorrow. Still, he wanted at least to feel and act like a regular boy, even if he had lost his innocence. So he joined a Jewish youth group, *Hashomer Hatzair*, in the Netherlands.

While he was there, Mathei learned the good news that his mother, brother, and sister had survived and were living in Romania. His father, as he suspected, was dead — a victim of Auschwitz. Mathei decided not to return to Romania, because he wanted to follow a new dream — a grand dream of being a part of something constructive, something worthwhile, something big.

In the fall of 1948, Mathei, now fourteen, arrived in his new adopted homeland. The country was Israel. The small nation was only five months old and in desperate need of young dreamers and hard workers, just like Mathei Jackel.

After becoming a citizen of Israel, Mathei joined the Israeli army and remained a soldier for many years. Then he started a second career as a physical education teacher. Today, Mathei lives on a kibbutz (a communal farm) in Israel. He is married and the father of two sons and a daughter.

More than thirty years after the war, Mathei's mother and siblings finally joined him in Israel.

No Wonder They Call This a Death March

Jack Gruener's Story

Jack Gruener tried not to wonder how he and 600 fellow prisoners were going to survive. Under heavy guard, they had just left Auschwitz in freezing weather on a forced march to Germany hundreds of miles away. As if that wasn't bad enough, all that each person had been given for food was one loaf of bread that had to last him the whole length of the two-week journey.

Jack, a seventeen-year-old Polish Jew, made sure his cold hands had a good grip around his two-and-a-half-pound (one-kilogram) loaf. *I must guard this with my life. I must be careful to eat only a little at a time, or I'll never make it. How is anyone supposed to survive? No wonder they call this a death march.*

The prisoners shuffled along in silence in two columns, holding their thin coats against the biting wind and clutching their loaves of bread. Rifle-toting SS guards and whip-cracking *kapos* walked along on either side, yelling at the prisoners and threatening them for not moving fast enough.

These prisoners had been teachers, doctors, musicians, and shopkeepers. The younger ones, like Jack, had been students. But that was five years and a lifetime ago, before the Nazis had stormed into Poland and made it a crime to be a Jew.

Now all the prisoners looked the same — like filthy, bald skeletons covered in lightweight striped prison uniforms. The lucky ones wore tattered coats or had rags to tie around their heads. The unlucky ones had lost their shoes and were forced to walk barefoot over the icy ground. These marchers were like thousands of other ragged prisoners being moved out of Polish death camps to Germany in the winter of 1945, as the Allied forces closed in on Poland.

I don't know how, but I'm going to survive, Jack promised himself. *I can't think any other way.*

The sound of a gunshot a few yards behind him broke into Jack's thoughts. He turned around to see a straggling prisoner fall dead at the feet of a Nazi, who held a smoking rifle.

"That's what will happen to us if we don't keep up," muttered a prisoner walking next to Jack. The sound of a gunshot was one Jack would hear often during the death march, but soon he didn't even bother to look.

For days, the weary group trudged through the snow on country roads, the winter wind stinging their gaunt faces. The Nazis wouldn't stop unless they found a place where they could easily guard the large group, so sometimes the prisoners had to walk for twenty hours straight before they were allowed to sleep.

On the fifth day, Jack glanced over at the prisoner staggering next to him. He was a boy younger than Jack. His face was red from fever, and his eyes were half shut.

He's going to die, Jack thought, and walked on a few steps, leaving the sick boy behind. Then Jack slowed down. *I don't want him to die.*

As the boy wobbled to the side, Jack saw a *kapo* coming up behind them. Jack figured that at any moment the boy would stumble and fall and then would be left on the side of the road with a bullet in his head, like so many other victims on this march.

Jack tucked his bread into the waistband of his pants. Turning to the boy, he said, "Come with me." Jack put his right arm around the boy's waist and draped the boy's bony left arm over his shoulders. Even though the boy was rail thin, lugging the extra weight quickly became almost too much to bear for Jack, who was only five feet three inches tall, and frail and weak himself.

With each step he took — each one harder than the one before — Jack questioned his own act of compassion. *What am I doing? Why am I carrying him along? I didn't think this through, and now I don't know how much longer I can do this. Maybe I should just let him go and save myself. But what if it was the other way around? What if he was dragging* me*? Would I want him to let me go?*

Prisoners were slogging past Jack because the extra

burden had slowed his pace. "Help me," Jack pleaded to the others. "Take his other arm. Please, please help."

But no one offered a hand.

"Leave him," grumbled a prisoner. "He's going to die anyway."

"Don't be a fool," another told Jack. "Let him go, or else he'll take you down with him."

At first Jack became angry, but part of him understood why no one wanted to help. It would take every ounce of strength to survive this brutal death march. A person had to think only of himself if he wanted to live. For a moment, he again considered slipping the boy's arm from around his shoulders, but a strong feeling deep inside Jack's soul kept him from doing it.

Although it was getting dark, the guards still hadn't found a safe place to stop, so the weary prisoners plodded on. Jack's shoulders ached and his legs quivered. But the worst agony was coming from his stomach. He was starving.

I wish I could get to my bread. Just one bite and then I'll be okay. But he couldn't free his hands to reach for the bread without dropping the boy. *If we stop, they'll shoot us. Maybe I should let him go. Then I could have a bite of bread. I'm so hungry, I can't stand it. How much longer can I go on like this?*

Then, all of sudden, Jack felt his load get lighter.

"I can't walk so well myself, but I'll help you," came a raspy voice from the darkening dusk. Jack glanced over and saw a middle-aged man with bloodshot eyes, deep lines in his face, and a grizzled beard. The man had grabbed the boy's other arm.

Together, the three moved on in silence. The only sounds were the crunching of footsteps on the frozen mud, the cracking of the *kapos'* whips, and the occasional loud bang of a gun as another straggler fell dead on the side of the road.

Finally, after the march reached the top of a steep hill, the guards ordered the prisoners to stop for the night. Jack and the older man gently dropped the boy, and then collapsed next to him. As soon as Jack's hand was free, he reached in his waistband for his bread. "My bread! It's gone!" he gasped, each word coming out in short, panicked bursts. Frantically, he felt all over his clothes for the half-eaten loaf. He got up and tried retracing his steps. *Where is it? If I've lost it, I'm a dead man.* His knees buckled, and he fell to the ground. He realized that he must have lost the bread along the way. *What am I going to do now?* Jack thought in despair.

The sick boy moaned. Jack crept over to see how he was doing and noticed a big piece of bread in his coat pocket. Jack slowly reached out to take it. *No, it's not right,* he told himself. Jack pulled his hand back and crawled away.

He flopped on the ground and tried to sleep, but he couldn't stop thinking about the bread in the boy's pocket. *He's so sick that he can't survive. If I take his bread, then at least I'll have a chance to live. Face it, he won't be able to walk anymore. He'll probably be dead by morning.* For three hours, Jack lay awake in the dark and cold, wrestling with his conscience. *I tried my best to save him, but he's going to die anyway, so I should take his bread. It's the only way I can survive. But can I really do that?*

By the first light of dawn, Jack had made his decision. He sneaked over to the boy, all the while hoping that he hadn't made it through the night so it wouldn't be a sin to steal his bread.

But the boy was breathing, and the redness in his face had gone. *He's alive! And he looks much better. Still, if it hadn't been for me . . .* Inch by inch, Jack slipped his hand into the boy's pocket and touched the bread. At that moment, the boy's eyes opened wide.

"Hey, what are you doing?" he said.

Jack jerked back his hand. "I just wanted to see if you were still alive, if you're okay," replied Jack. The boy grunted and fell back asleep.

I can't do it, Jack said to himself. *I can't take his bread.*

Later in the morning, when the grueling march began again, the boy was able to walk on his own. Jack stayed alongside him for a while but eventually lost sight of him when the boy slowed down. By now, Jack wasn't thinking about the boy anymore. All that was on his mind was how stupid he had been, and how hard he had struggled to stay alive ever since the Germans invaded Poland. For more than five years he had cheated death, and now he was angry with himself for being so foolish on this death march. *After everything I've gone through, I'm going to die now because I lost my bread.*

⧖   ⧖   ⧖

Jack was twelve when the Germans raised the Nazi flag over Krakow, Poland, on September 6, 1939. He watched in horror as some of his neighbors rushed out into the streets to greet the invaders, not realizing that the arrival of these soldiers would mean death for millions of Polish people.

What's wrong with them? Jack thought. *Don't they know what's going to happen?*

He had heard bits of conversations between adults in the street as he walked to school or to the library. Much of the talk centered on the Nazis' determination to wipe out all Jews.

At the library, Jack read lots of newspaper articles about the Nazis. He learned that in Germany, Jews had lost everything — their jobs, their homes, and sometimes their lives. There was little reason to hope that the Jews of Krakow wouldn't soon suffer the same cruel treatment.

Jack loved the library because there was so much to learn — some of it bad, much of it good. He read stories about the Indians, who lived far away in a fascinating land called America. He read books on medicine and science, and enjoyed learning about how things worked. Jack was especially intrigued by electricity.

For about a month after the German occupation began, Jack's life remained fairly normal. Then the Nazis started issuing new orders to the Jews in Krakow: "No Jew can use the sidewalk." "All Jews must tip their hats to German officers." "Jews must clean the snow from the streets." Soon, Jews had no rights at all. Jewish children were expelled from school, and all Jews were barred from the library — an edict that particularly pained Jack. Meanwhile, more than 35,000 Jews were forced to leave the city.

In March 1941, the Nazis ordered 20,000 Jews — one third of the city's Jewish population — to move into Podgorze, a small district of Krakow. The Nazis then made the Jews build a high cement wall topped with barbed wire to seal them into this ghetto. No one could get out without a special pass.

In the ghetto, Jack, his mother, Mina, and his father, Oskar, who was forced to give up his shoe business, were supposed to share a three-room apartment in a three-story building with twelve other people. But Jack had a better idea. In a space above the top floor, he discovered a steel door that looked similar to the kind used on a bank vault. It was unlocked. When Jack opened it, he stepped into a room filled with feathers and filth.

Jack ran downstairs and brought his father back. "I don't know what this was," Jack said, "maybe a pigeon coop or a place where the building's owner kept his valuables hidden. It doesn't matter. We could clean this up so the three of us could live here. It will be better than living with all those other people in that apartment."

"You're right, Jackie," his father said. "There's no bathroom here, but we can use the one in the apartment. I'm glad you found this."

The Grueners scrubbed the walls and floors of the pigeon coop and dragged in mattresses, chairs, and lamps. They hung a blackout curtain over the one window so no one could see them from the outside. Using the knowledge of electricity he had gained from his research in the library and from a friend who was an electrician, Jack wired the room so his family would have light and be able to cook on a hot plate.

Jack and Oskar also installed four heavy iron bars that fit across the steel door to help prevent the Gestapo from breaking in. The Grueners had heard that the Nazis were sweeping through towns, grabbing anyone they could for deportation to camps, such as Auschwitz, which was only forty miles (sixty-four kilometers) away. The Nazis claimed these *aktzias* were necessary because the Germans needed workers for the war effort. But many of the Jews who were taken to Auschwitz were never heard from again.

More than 6,000 Jews had disappeared in the first *aktzia*, in May 1941. Five months later, rumors spread that another round of deportations was on the way. "They want thousands, they will take everyone," a friend warned Jack. "It will be the biggest *aktzia* yet."

When word spread throughout the ghetto, many Jews went into hiding, including seven of Jack's aunts, uncles, and cousins, who joined his family in their safe room. So many Jews were hiding that it became difficult for the Nazis to fill their quota, which angered the Gestapo.

"If we sit in this room and lock this door, I'm sure nobody will be able to break in," Jack told his relatives when the *aktzia* began. Soon, they heard gunfire and screaming in the streets. Jack peeked out the window and saw Gestapo officers machine-gunning ill and elderly patients from the hospital next door.

For two days, Jack and his family huddled in the darkened room in silence. Not a word was uttered, especially when they heard Nazi soldiers rattling the door, shaking it harder and harder, trying to open it until finally giving up.

On the evening of the second day, Jack heard loud-speakers on trucks driving through the ghetto announce: "Everyone is ordered to assemble in the streets immediately. If you don't come out by six P.M., you will be shot on sight."

In the Gruener hideout, Uncle Moshe started walking toward the door, saying, "We have to go now. Why be killed?"

"No!" Jack shouted. "It's a trick to get us to come out. I'm not going."

"What do you know? You're just a boy! We must go and take our chances . . . or they'll kill us all right here."

Soon everyone was arguing. In tears, Jack leaped up, pulled back the iron bars, and flung open the door. "If you want to go, then leave right now. But I'm not going. It's almost certain death out there. At least we'll be safe in here."

His family stared at him for a few moments. Then his parents stood up and said, "We're not going." One by one, the other family members agreed to stay, even Uncle Moshe. Jack closed the door and slid the bars across again, locking everyone in.

They sat quietly, listening to the horrible sounds of the brutality outside. Two days later, the streets were calm. Their quota filled, the Nazis left everyone else alone. Jack learned later that everyone who had been picked up had gone straight to the Birkenau death camp and was gassed.

The following week, Jack saw his mother ripping open a seam in the sleeve of his father's brown coat. "What are you doing?" he asked.

"I'm putting two thousand *zlotys* in your father's coat and sewing it up. I've already hidden the same amount in the sleeve of your gray coat. That way, if we ever escape, we'll have some money. We'll keep the coats here until we need them. Don't forget."

A few weeks later, Jack visited a friend on the other side of the ghetto. On his way back, he saw the Gestapo loading several Jews onto a truck in front of his apartment building. It was a sad sight Jack had seen too many times before. Afraid they might grab him, too, he waited behind a corner until the truck left.

When he arrived in the attic room, he found his cousin Sala weeping in the corner. "Jackie, the Nazis grabbed your mother and father! They had gone for food and were entering the building just a few minutes ago when the Gestapo took them away."

Jack doubled over and fell to his knees. "Noooo!" he wailed.

One by one, the Gestapo picked up every member of his family, until he was the only one left. Jack started taking chances, like not wearing his Star of David and slipping out of the ghetto through a tiny hole in the wall. With his blond hair and "Aryan" features, he easily passed for a non-Jew and was able to walk the streets of Krakow without raising suspicion. He thought about heading into the woods and hiding out on a farm. But, afraid of what the Gestapo would do if they caught him, he always returned to the ghetto.

Unfortunately, less than a year later, Jack was nabbed by German soldiers, forced into a truck jammed with other frightened Jews, and driven out of the ghetto. Although only fifteen, he was strong, and the Nazis needed good workers. So Jack was sent outside Krakow to the Plaszow forced-labor camp, which was built on a site that was once a Jewish cemetery. For Jack, the only good thing about the camp was that he could spend some time with Uncle Moshe, who had been sent there months earlier.

Every day was filled with backbreaking labor, but even worse was the terror dealt by the camp's evil commandant, Amon Goeth.

"The man is crazy," Uncle Moshe told Jack when he arrived. "He has no soul. He'll kill a man just as easily as if he were swatting a fly. Whenever he has nothing to do in his villa — the one overlooking the camp — he plays music while shooting a prisoner or two with his high-powered rifle. When you see Goeth, you see death."

On work details, Jack trembled every time he saw Goeth, a tall man with an icy stare. With another SS officer on one side and a fierce German shepherd on the other, Goeth would strut around camp in his high black boots. He would inspect his ragged captives as they hauled and dug, each of them trying to avoid his gaze.

The first time Jack was on a work detail digging a

trench, Goeth came up to the prisoner who was overseeing the project and asked, "How much did your group do to-day?"

"We've completed six trenches, sir."

"You didn't do enough!" Goeth screamed. He took the leash off one of his massive dogs, pointed at the overseer, and, with a wicked smile, shouted to the dog, *"Jude!"* (the German word for Jew). With a growl, the enormous animal bared its teeth and leaped on top of the overseer. Jack closed his eyes, but he couldn't block out the sound of the man's screams.

The next day, Jack's group worked even harder under a new overseer. Late in the day, Goeth asked the overseer, "How much was done today?"

In a frightened voice, the overseer replied, "Ten trenches, sir."

Goeth bellowed, "You must be lying! No group could dig that many in a day!" He pulled out a pistol and shot him.

This maniac murdered so many inmates that the prisoners started to keep a daily tally, as if it were a ghoulish ball game. Whenever the prisoners returned to the barracks from a work detail, they would ask grimly, "What's the score today?"

Because he was petrified of Goeth, Jack always volunteered for work outside the camp, figuring he had a better chance of avoiding the madman.

He was part of a work detail that spent days cleaning the

Krakow ghetto, which was liquidated, or emptied, of the remaining Jews in March 1943. Thousands of Jews were forced to leave behind their belongings, which were strewn around the streets.

While sorting through a pile of clothes near his former apartment building, Jack came across a familiar brown coat. *This looks just like Papa's. Could it be his?* Jack checked inside the sleeve and gasped when he saw stitching and felt a tell-tale lump underneath. *I've found Papa's coat! The money is still in it!*

He rummaged through the pile, hoping to find his gray coat. Minutes later . . . *There it is! I can't believe my great luck! This is amazing!* He felt the lump in the sleeve. *The money!*

When no one was looking, Jack threw off the coat he was wearing and put on his old gray coat. Then, checking again to make sure he wasn't seen, he ripped the money out of his father's coat and stuffed it into the other sleeve of his own coat. *With this money I can buy soap and extra food and smuggle it back into camp. I can use it to bribe guards, too, for some favors.*

Later that afternoon, as members of the work detail were about to board trucks to go back to camp, the SS guards announced that if anyone had found any money while going through abandoned belongings in the ghetto, he had to turn it over. Jack watched as one prisoner, who had been caught hiding a few coins that he had found, was shot.

"If you have any money, you'd better give it up now or you'll be executed, too," an SS officer told the prisoners.

What should I do? wondered Jack. *I have all these zlotys in my sleeve. But if I rip the money out of my coat and give it to them, they're likely to shoot me anyway.*

"This is your last call," said the officer. "Whoever has money, show it now."

Don't say anything and hope they don't check my sleeves.

They didn't. But Jack knew Goeth would order a search of all the prisoners later. When he returned to the camp, he told Uncle Moshe about the money. Moshe took the money and promised to find a good hiding spot. He would tell Jack the secret location the next time they met.

A few days later, Jack returned to the barracks from the work detail in the ghetto and asked Fred, a friend of his, "So, what's the score today?"

"One man," replied Fred, turning his head away so Jack wouldn't see his eyes.

The way he answered made Jack uneasy. "Is it somebody I know?" When his friend didn't reply, Jack grabbed his shoulders and demanded, "Tell me, Fred, who was it?"

"While you were working in the ghetto, your uncle Moshe was overseeing a work crew here. Goeth walked by and asked him how much his group had done. I'm sorry, Jack. Goeth didn't like his answer."

That night, Jack lay on his bunk, wondering how much more hurt he could bear. *Everyone I love has been murdered or taken away. Now Uncle Moshe has been killed. And I never even got the chance to find out where he hid the money.*

Jack was feeling hopeless. His arm dangled over the side of the lower bunk, and his fingers aimlessly swept back and forth along the floor. Suddenly, he felt that one of the floorboards was loose. When no one was looking, he pulled up the board and two other loose ones and peered underneath to see a small crawl space big enough to hold three inmates his size. Then he replaced the boards and ran to tell Fred and their friend Isaac about his discovery.

The next morning, as the other prisoners filed out the door to go to work, the boys lifted the boards and slipped under the barracks. They talked a little, but mostly they slept and let their weakened bodies rest. They crawled out just before the exhausted workers returned to the barracks that evening.

They hid like this every day for two weeks, until one afternoon . . .

"I hear voices," Jack whispered to his two pals. He peeked through a small crack between the barracks and the ground. What he saw sent shock waves of panic through his body. "It's Goeth with two guards and one of his killer dogs. They're heading toward our barracks."

"That dog will smell us," gasped Fred. "We're going to be killed."

Isaac broke into a sweat. "What will we do?"

Jack looked through the gap again. They were getting closer, and the dog had lifted its ears and was staring straight in Jack's direction. Jack had to think fast. "Before they get here, let's hurry up and get out and pretend we're on a work detail."

"But they'll kill us," Isaac said.

"We're all but dead now anyway," said Jack. "Either we'll be killed, or we won't." He could hear Goeth's voice getting louder. "There's no time to spare."

The three boys squeezed out from under the loose boards, replaced them, and left the barracks through the back door. They walked around to the front of the building and directly toward Goeth, the guards, and the German shepherd.

"Stop!" Goeth yelled. "Where are you going?"

"We're going to a work detail at the south side of the camp, sir," Jack said, trying to disguise the fear in his voice. The dog stood by Goeth's side and let out a growl. Goeth glared at Jack for a moment and then, without a word, walked away.

"Let's go," Jack said to his friends, and the relieved trio headed to the other side of the camp. They never again hid under the barracks.

A few months later, Jack and about 800 other prisoners began a strenuous odyssey. They were put on trucks and sent from one camp to another, wherever slave labor was needed to aid the Nazi war effort. They cut wood, dug ditches, hauled stones, and crushed rocks into gravel. The camps blended together in Jack's mind, as he went from one torturous job to the next, with little to eat other than watery soup and stale bread.

It was a struggle to work, and an even greater struggle to keep hope alive. Over and over, Jack saw prisoners die within days of giving up, and every time he saw them fall, he'd promise himself, *I'm going to fight for my life*. All the horror just made him want to live that much more. *I know that there will be a better world when this war is over. It won't always be this bad.*

Each of the camps held its own terrors. Jack realized that for the black-hearted guards, killing was an enjoyable pastime, like playing cards. They murdered for fun, often making prisoners dig their own graves before they were shot. Jack was as angry as he was scared — angry at these monsters and, in some ways, even more angry at the prisoners who meekly followed, with heads bowed, the ghoulish orders leading to their own execution.

No one is going to do that to me. I'll kick the guards in the shins and run. I won't go like a sheep to the slaughter.

But sometimes the best course of action was to do nothing. One day, a large, beefy *kapo* named Moonface spotted Jack walking in the camp. The *kapo* was called Moonface (but only out of earshot) because he had a huge round head. Moonface had been in a civilian prison on a murder charge, but when the Nazis took over Poland, he was sent to the concentration camp and made a *kapo*.

"Come over here," Moonface ordered Jack. When Jack did as he was told, the *kapo* punched him in the face.

"What was that for?" Jack cried out, wincing in pain. "What did I do?"

"You looked at me the wrong way."

Jack seldom looked at him again. Instead, he worked harder every time Moonface was around.

At another camp, the guards made a sport of finding excuses to hang prisoners. One day, the guards grabbed five men who were working outside the camp and accused them of plotting an escape. The rest of the inmates in camp were forced to watch as the noose was slipped around the necks of the five doomed prisoners and, one by one, they were dropped to their deaths. Seconds before the last was hanged, he looked at the crowd and declared, "I never tried to escape. I am innocent. Remember that."

I'll remember, Jack thought. *I'll remember.*

Each morning that Jack woke up was another victory, another day he didn't face death from a trumped-up charge or from giving the wrong answer or from going into a shower that spewed poison gas instead of water.

◎   ◎   ◎

Jack had gone through so much in all the camps. Now, here he was in January 1945, at the end of the first week of this death march, dying from hunger because he had foolishly lost his bread while trying to help a stranger.

As Jack plodded along, wondering how much time he had left before he keeled over from lack of food, he spotted Moonface. The man was vicious, but when Jack saw that Moonface had four large round loaves of bread slung over his back, Jack decided the *kapo* was his only hope.

Maybe he'll remember that I'm a good worker, Jack thought. *Maybe he'll give me some bread.*

The rest of the day, Jack made sure that Moonface noticed him by walking in front of him or near his side. When Moonface walked quickly, Jack made his feet move faster, too, even if it hurt. He stayed close to the *kapo* until the march stopped for the night.

When Moonface took off his backpack and reached for one of his loaves, Jack inched closer. He looked around to see if there were any other *kapos* in the area, because if there were, there was a good chance Moonface would beat him to impress the others with his toughness. Jack didn't see any other *kapos*, though, just the worn, tired bodies of prisoners slumped over on the ground.

It's time to make my move, Jack told himself. *I don't care what happens. If he beats me or kills me for what I'm about to ask, it doesn't make any difference, because I'm dead anyway without something to eat.*

Jack walked with strong steps to Moonface and looked into his cruel black eyes.

"Do you remember me?" Jack asked.

Moonface grunted.

"Then you know I am a good worker," Jack said in a firm voice. Other prisoners who were watching nearby expected the worst. They were sure this huge man would kill the brave teenager for even talking to him. "I want to work, but I'm not going to survive this march much longer without some bread," Jack continued. "I lost mine, and I was hoping you could give me some. I am a good worker."

Moonface scowled as he pulled out his knife and pointed it at Jack. The other prisoners cringed and held their breath, anticipating a quick, fatal slash across Jack's throat. Jack studied Moonface's expression, trying to get a clue to what was going through the *kapo's* mind. *Is he thinking of helping me or killing me? Whatever it is, he should just get it over with.*

Moonface raised his knife, then sliced a good chunk

off the loaf he held in his hand and tossed it to Jack. A murmur of relief rippled through the prisoners, but it was cut short when Moonface glared at them.

Jack wanted to bite into the bread and devour all of it right away, but he knew that he had to be careful, to take just as much as he needed. It had to last him for another week. He broke off a small piece and put it in his mouth. Never was there anything that tasted so good.

When they finally reached the German border, the prisoners were put into open boxcars for a three-day trip to a camp at Sachsenhausen. It snowed during the trip, but at least they didn't have to walk anymore, and the snow gave them something to drink. Unfortunately, they had little to eat in the camp before they were sent a few weeks later to another camp, where they were supposed to help repair a bombed-out Messerschmitt fighter-plane factory.

By the time they arrived, scores of prisoners were too weak to stand. "You brought me dead people," the camp commandant complained to the *kapos.* "How can they help rebuild this factory in their condition?"

The commandant told his men to pick out the weakest prisoners and get rid of them. About seventy-five prisoners were taken off to the side and shot.

"Now, the others will need a week to recuperate. Give them good food and let them rest," he ordered.

The camp kitchen turned out a rich, thick soup, with meat and vegetables, the first that Jack had tasted in years. He savored the smell in his bowl and then devoured the soup, along with a big piece of bread. But in less than an hour, his stomach felt as if it was on fire. Everyone was suffering from cramps.

From his days of reading books about medicine in the Krakow library, Jack figured out that after being starved for so long, his stomach couldn't handle the rich soup. He remembered reading how to cure these painful cramps.

He traded his soup for bread and toasted it over a pot-bellied stove in the barracks. For the whole week that the other prisoners ate the soup and got sick, Jack continued to eat only the toasted bread and soon cured himself. It was difficult for him to pass up the soup, but he knew he had to do it to survive.

When it was determined that the airplane factory was beyond repair, Jack and the other prisoners were shipped to the camp in Bergen-Belsen, which by now had become horribly overcrowded. At night, the prisoners were squeezed so tightly into the barracks that the guards had to push them in with sticks. No one could lie down. They had to squat, knees out to the side. Every day, as more prisoners died, new ones were stuffed into the barracks.

Jack heard a rumor that the Nazis needed workers at a small camp and were using a test to pick only the strongest and healthiest among the frail prisoners. For the test, each inmate who wanted to work had to take off his clothes, roll them in a bundle under his arm, and dash through a barracks in front of three SS officers, who would decide if he seemed physically able to work.

Jack desperately wanted to work because it meant leaving Bergen-Belsen, so he showed up for the test. When it was his turn, he stripped and was shocked to see just how scrawny he was. His skin was gray and blotchy, his arms and legs like toothpicks. He couldn't worry about how he looked. He had a test to pass. To fail now meant he would almost certainly die in Bergen-Belsen.

"You!" an SS officer screamed. "Run!" Jack started with a jolt, running as fast as he could through the barracks, running for his life. When he reached the other side, he was exhausted and wanted to lie down so the burning sensation in his legs and lungs would go away. Instead, he stood erect, as though he had just finished a stroll in the park.

"He can work," the officer announced.

Jack and about 400 others who passed the test were loaded onto cattle cars for a three-day trip to the other camp. But when they arrived, they found that there was no work to do, so the Nazis moved them to Dachau — Jack's tenth camp — where the only work was trying to stay alive.

Shortly after his arrival, Jack was jarred awake at about 2 A.M. by deafening blasts. For the next several hours, planes roared overhead and artillery fire and shells whizzed around the camp and exploded nearby, shaking the barracks. The Americans were attacking German gunnery units, and the camp was caught in the crossfire.

There was nothing the inmates could do to protect themselves. They had to stay put in the camp and hope that no bombs or shells would land on their barracks. *I don't believe this,* Jack thought. *I've survived all these years, and now I might get killed right here, just days away from being liberated! So this is how life is. Sometimes things happen at the right time. Sometimes they happen at the wrong time.*

Eventually, everything went quiet, except for the thud of distant guns. At dawn, an inmate crept out of the barracks. "There are no guards! There are no guards!" he yelled. "The Nazis are gone!"

Slowly, Jack and the rest of the prisoners walked out into the sunlight. The watchtowers were empty. The soldiers had vanished. The prisoners kept looking around, wondering what was happening. And then, as their minds slowly grasped the fact that they were free, they began to grin and say prayers of thanksgiving.

Off in the distance, Jack spotted a tank rumbling up the road. It sported a red-white-and-blue flag on the side. "The Americans are coming! The Americans are coming!" Jack shouted in sharp, raspy cries of joy. He knew then that he had made it, just as he had promised himself he would. Jack Gruener had survived.

❀

After the war ended, the Supreme National Tribunal in Poland found Amon Goeth guilty of killing 500 Jewish prisoners. He was hanged for his crimes in Krakow in 1946.

Meanwhile, Jack went back to Krakow looking for his parents, but he never learned what had happened to them. He assumed they had been killed. He and two cousins were the only family members who survived the war. Jack visited with one of the cousins, who was living in Munich,

Germany. While in Munich, Jack met Luncia Gamzer — whose story as a hidden child begins this book — and he stayed in touch with her after he emigrated to New York in 1948.

A year later, Luncia and her parents settled in Brooklyn, New York. Jack began dating Luncia, who had changed her name to Ruth, and they married in 1953. Together they built a successful interior-design firm and raised two sons — Daniel, a doctor, and Arthur, a lawyer — and have four grandchildren.

Today, Jack and Ruth, who live in Brooklyn, give talks about their Holocaust experiences at every opportunity, especially to schoolchildren, in the hope that people will remember what happened . . . and keep it from happening again.

Glossary

aktzia (**ahkt**-zee-ah; Polish): the rounding up of Jews for deportation or execution

appell (ah-**pell**; German): roll call

Babcia (**bahb**-chuh; Polish): Grandma

Gestapo (ge-**shta**-poh; German): the police force of the Nazi Party

Judenrat (**yoo**-den-raht; German): a Jewish council appointed to carry out Nazi orders within a Jewish community

kapo (**kah**-poh; German): a concentration-camp guard or policeman; *kapos* were selected from among the inmates, and many had criminal backgrounds

Kindertransport (**kin**-der-**trans**-port; German): an organization that worked to remove Jewish children from Nazi-occupied countries and bring them to safety

Kristallnacht (krist-**ahl**-nacht; German): Night of Broken Glass; specifically, the night of November 9 and 10, 1938, when Nazi-backed mobs throughout Germany and Austria attacked Jews in the street, in their homes, and at their places of work and worship

Mamusia (ma-**moo**-shah; Polish): Mama

muselmann (**moo**-zel-mahn; German): a concentration-camp inmate close to death

Mutti (**moo**-ti; German): Mommy

Nazi (**nah**-tsi; German): a member of the National Socialist Party, which ruled Germany from 1933 to 1945 under Adolf Hitler

SS: abbreviation for *Schutzstaffel*, an elite German military unit serving Hitler and the Nazi Party during World War II

Sternlager (**shtairn**-lah-ger; German): Star Camp; a more privileged section of Bergen-Belsen concentration camp for those with connections in the United States

Tate (**tah**-teh; Yiddish): Papa

Tatu (**tah**-too; Polish): Papa

Torah (**toe**-rah; Hebrew): a sacred scroll of the Five Books of Moses

zlotys (**zlo**-teez): Polish currency